TURNAROUND ARTISTS

By Ahad Ghadimi

TURNAROUND ARTISTS
Published by Forums@Work Publishing™
Copyright © 2020 Ahad Ghadimi

Cover design by Chiara Ghigliazza
Layout design by Eled Cernik

Printed in the United States of America

ISBN: 978-0-578-80512-2

Dedicated to the men and women who work on the frontlines of business.

From restaurants and hotels, to grocery stores, medical clinics and the manufacturing floor - I've witnessed the incredible effort you contribute and the massive challenges of your work environment.

I have enormous respect and admiration for what you do.

This book is to celebrate, empower and support you.

Table of Contents

Prologue

Eddie Jr.'s eyes were fixed on the door as he waited for the slightest hint of activity. He held his breath so that he could hear better.

He sat so far on the edge of the couch that he was in danger of falling off. His attention was fixed, his feet in a runner's block position, one slightly in front of the other.

Getting this far had taken lengthy lobbying of his mother until she finally relented and allowed him to stay up just a little later than usual to show his father his homework. It was a science project he had been working on for several days, and he was more proud of it than anything he had ever done.

Staying up late didn't come cheap, but his mother could see how much it meant to him. Still, Eddie Jr. had only secured the coveted bedtime extension with future promises that involved good behavior and consuming all his vegetables at dinner.

Now all he had to do was wait, eyes fixed on the clock as it ticked painfully slow, second by second, toward the moment when his father would finally be home. Eight years old, Eddie had recently learned to read time; after tracking it for several weeks, he knew that 8:48 PM was typically when he heard the keys jingle outside their apartment door.

The entire evening had been building up to this moment. Eddie Jr. strained his ears, his acute attention helping him distinguish between the harsh noise of the rough neighborhood outside which had become the wallpaper of their life in that tiny apartment - and the all important sound of the keys.

Finally, there it was, the jingle of his father's keys. Eddie readied himself. As the lock turned, he bolted down the hallway toward the front door, stopping midway with his homework clutched proudly in his hand.

The door opened and his father stepped inside. His heavy, battered leather briefcase was clutched tightly in one hand, keys in the other, a perpetual frown drawing his thick eyebrows together.

"Look what I did, Daddy!" Junior blurted out as soon as his father had closed the door.

His father turned his fierce gaze on his son.

"What the hell are you still doing up?" he growled, pushing past without even a glance at the homework.

"I wanted to show you my - "

"Get to bed! Maureen, what the hell is he still doing up?"

He stomped into the kitchen, dropped his briefcase on the table and slumped into a chair, still wearing his coat. His eyes were tired as he gazed into nowhere, his mind churning.

Eddie Jr. still stood in the hallway, frozen by his father's disdain.

His mother glanced at her son, a look of devastated disappointment on his face, then at Edward Sr.

"That seemed a bit harsh, dear. Edddie waited up just to see you. He idolizes you."

"I've told you a hundred times, he shouldn't be up past his bedtime." He barked, then sighed deeply and focused his eyes on his wife, who stood in the doorway trying to bridge the gap between father and son. "Things aren't good. I fired Daphne today. I'm going to have to go in early tomorrow to open the store."

Eddie Jr. took a couple of steps toward the kitchen, uncertain what to do. His mother saw him out of the corner of her eye and briefly shook her head, gesturing for him to go to his room. Still clutching his homework, Eddie slipped away with shoulders down and feet dragging, one weary, disappointed step at a time, desperately hoping to be called back. He paused in the doorway to his room, his parents' voices carrying to him.

"But you're already working 12-hour days - you can't carry on this way, dear. Why don't you call your father? Maybe he can give you some advice."

"To hell with his advice. I don't need his help. I told you, I'm going to make this place a success. Get us out of this joke of an apartment and into a real home. I'll show him - I don't need anyone."

Junior realized there was to be no reprieve. He closed his bedroom door, slumped onto his bed and sobbed.

Author's Introduction

Why I wrote this book

G rowing up, I truly believed accolades and big accomplishments would fill the void of worthiness and meaning in my life, so I feverishly sought them out. Fresh after graduating from one of the top undergraduate business schools in the world, I moved to Costa Rica and co-founded a women's swimsuit line with a former Miss France. Within our first year, we were featured in the iconic *Sports Illustrated Swimsuit Issue* and every other fashion magazine on the newsstand from *Vogue*, to *InStyle* to *Women's Wear Daily*. We quickly became the swimsuit of choice for the A-list (and famously denied making Ricky Martin a male version of our suits).

From there, my life was filled with many exciting and rich chapters. I transitioned from the wild and colorful world of fashion to the heights of corporate France. In Paris's tony Opera neighborhood, I was named the Worldwide Training Manager for Groupe Danone before my 25th birthday, leading innovation, culture and change management across 111 countries and 95,000 employees globally. Ten years later, I held CEO roles and ownership stakes in a portfolio of companies totaling over $30MM in revenue. I had fulfilled a long-held dream of being a turnaround artist – the person who swoops in to fix troubled businesses. It felt like there was nothing I couldn't do. Impressive on LinkedIn, grist for cocktail party conversation - it painted the picture of an accomplished life. Amidst it all, however, no matter which exotic place I lived in or exciting project I was leading, I had a profound feeling of isolation...

Little did I know that I was not alone in feeling this way, but it took an invitation to join YPO (Young Presidents Organization) to open my eyes. I had first heard about YPO as a teenager from a mentor who was a member. YPO is an ultra-exclusive members' organization for people who hold the role of CEO/President of mid-to-large size companies before their 45th birthday. It has a considerable caché and cool factor.

Within months of becoming a member, I enjoyed exclusive YPO experiences like getting special access to a dozen country Presidents at UN Week in New York, an intimate fireside hangout with Lance Armstrong, and playing poker beside Flava Flav in a game run by Molly Bloom in West Hollywood. However, while many people are initially attracted to YPO membership because of its prestige, the reason most people renew their annual membership is because of their Forum.

Life after joining the YPO Forum

The Forum set-up is pretty simple. YPO members are placed in a group with seven to nine other CEOs and meet monthly for four hours to share about their business, personal, and family lives. Specifically, we talk about the good, the bad and the ugly - otherwise known as the top 5% and bottom 5% of what we are dealing with in all aspects of our lives. From multimillion-dollar business exits to being diagnosed with cancer and to infidelity, your Forum will typically know more about you than anyone else on Earth. The commitment is strict. If you miss two sessions you are automatically kicked out - even being late to a meeting could cost you up to $1,000 a minute.

For me, Forum meetings were life changing indeed - at my first Forum session, I had a major "Aha!" moment.

When I first joined YPO, I was the youngest person in my Chapter. The achievements of my Forum-mates were literally out-of-this-world (one person was launching satellites into space – and that was just one of their many businesses). Leading up to our first meeting, I was so nervous about having to open up and be vulnerable with my new peers that I almost skipped the session altogether. Imagine worrying that your coveted YPO membership might be revoked because of your fears and insecurities.

My first meeting was in a boardroom atop one of Denver's downtown towers. The blinds to the meeting room were drawn and a handwritten sign on the door read DO NOT DISTURB. The seven of us sat in a circle. I sat and listened as other Forum members spoke about the highs and lows of their personal and professional lives. I could relate to so much of what they were sharing; I was frankly surprised that other CEOs *at this level* were facing the same kinds of challenges as me. I was the last to share. When my turn came, my face was hot, my heart pounded and I felt as if I was on a choppy boat ride while my new Forum-mates looked at me and said, "You're up."

Despite my fears, I dove in and talked about what was going well and also about a few issues I was running into. It felt like middle-of-the road stuff, and I couldn't help but think about how my Forum-mates had revealed incredibly personal and private details of their lives. Yet here I was, faking it, feeling less than candid, not *authentic*.

I stopped and took a deep breath. *There was no point in doing this if I didn't do it properly,* I told myself. Everyone was looking at me. It was now or never.

"Alright. I'm going to level with you guys," I announced. "I am having a really hard time with a deal I am working on. In fact, I'm so stuck, I have no idea what to do."

Encouraged by the interested faces that stared back at me, I took the plunge and truly got into the *bottom five percent* of my business – everything that was going wrong. I spoke about the things I really struggled with in my personal and family life. I spilled it all out, wondering every second if it was the right thing to do.

When I finally finished I sat back and wondered what would happen next. The silence that comes after spilling your guts can feel like an eternity. Like skydiving, I had taken the plunge and I was now free-falling. Would there be a parachute, or just the brutality of crashing into the ground at high speed?

Then one of my Forum-mates nodded and said, "Oh, I've definitely been there – and more than once."

Another Forum-mate sighed and raised her hand. "Yep, dealing with something similar right now. Let's talk about this more – I'm stuck also."

I tried in vain to keep the grin of relief from my face. I was not alone!

What I felt that evening is impossible to capture in words, though I will never forget it. When I left, I felt elated and euphoric. Instead of taking an Uber, I walked- practically floated- the 40 minutes home on that brisk Colorado evening, wondering:

"What if I had skipped the meeting?"

"How would I have known that what I was dealing with wasn't 'just me'?"

"How long would I have needlessly beaten myself up over it?"

"How different would my life have been had I joined a Forum sooner?"

I had my first taste of being in a Forum. I had taken the first, tentative step out of isolation and into feeling connection and community with others like me. The more I thought about it, the more I saw the enormous benefits this would have for people, businesses, and society at large.

That night, as I lay in bed, my head still spun. I thought, *"If CEOs of big companies rely on this type of support and the*

opportunity to be vulnerable to help them with their lives, what is
everyone else supposed to do?"

By being in a Forum, I had *experienced* first hand how my peers shared "my" problems and how having a truly safe space to share these experiences could transform a life. The more I thought about it, the more I wanted to find a way to share this experience, this awesome resource, with other people. And so was born the idea of writing this book.

> **"**
>
> *Not everything that is faced can be changed. But nothing can be changed until it is faced.*
>
> JAMES BALDWIN
>
> **"**

CHAPTER 1

A Family Feud

E ddie hurried into the office, eager to get back to work. His face was tanned, and despite a bit of jet lag, he felt energized, ready. People called out to him as he strode through to his office.

"Hey Ed, how was the vacation?"

"You're in one piece!"

"Welcome back!"

Eddie settled into his chair. Everything looked normal, familiar. It was hard to believe that just over 24 hours ago he had been skiing in Val d'Isère, high in the French Alps.

He had barely fired up his laptop before his business partner, Chris, was in his office, two steaming cups of coffee in his hands.

After a few minutes of casual conversation, he got down to business. "The Campbell deal is still in the balance," he told Eddie. "I think you need to fly to San Francisco again to get this deal over the line."

Eddie sighed. He'd been looking forward to a few quiet days in the office to get caught up. "If that's what it takes."

Chris laughed as he stood up. "Don't pretend you don't love it. Lunch at Fisherman's Wharf? Dinner in the Mission?"

Eddie grinned. "If I have to."

"I'll let them know you're coming and have Josie make your reservations. Wednesday good for you?"

"Sure."

Chris hurried out, leaving Eddie to catch his breath for a minute. He had barely started going through his emails when his phone rang. He glanced at the screen: Mom.

Eddie knew why she was calling. His father had been in a car accident while Eddie was away and was laid up with a broken leg. Eddie had promised to get up to see them as soon as he could, but with the trip to San Francisco now on his agenda, it was going to be the weekend at the earliest before he could do so.

"Hi Mom."

"Eddie dear? It's your momma."

"Yes, Mom. How's Dad?"

"Annoying. Frustrating. Grumpy."

"So no change from normal, then?"

"He's worried about the restaurant. He's been out for over a week. He's fretting and fussing - wants you to come keep an eye on it until he's back on his feet."

"Not happening, Mom. They'll be fine. They're all grown-ups. They know what to do without Dad hovering over them every minute of the day. He's talking to Olga, right?"

"All day, every day. I'm surprised the woman has the time to get anything done."

Eddie sighed, rubbing his forehead. He was not in the mood for this and didn't have time for it, especially right now.

"Mom, I just got back into the office. I need to get some work done. I'll try and get down for a visit this weekend," he promised.

Despite his mom's protests, Eddie managed to end the call and get stuck into his own work, but he already had a knot in his gut at the thought of talking to his father. He had grown up with his father's micro-management, had seen what it had done to the restaurant's employees, to his family. There was no way he was going to step into that hornet's nest.

San Francisco was as delightful as ever. The city had a vibrancy that Eddie fed off of, a combination of the big city bustle and the sea air. And as Chris had suggested, he had lunch at Fisherman's Wharf, sitting on the terrace eating fresh lobster and watching sailboats bob on gentle waves, their lines chiming gently against masts. He had a three o'clock meeting with their clients, just enough time for a quick stroll before taking a taxi to Richmond. Eddie needed time to clear his head and think about the meeting. Eddie's business consisted of buying businesses from retiring business owners and transitioning them into employee-owned enterprises; while some couldn't wait to retire and leave the stress behind them, others, like their client in San Francisco, struggled to actually let go of the strings. As Eddie stood up from the table, his phone buzzed as it did 50 times a day.

Mom.

Again.

"Hi Mom. What's today's emergency?"

"Olga just called me."

"She called you directly? And?"

"She says it's chaos. Your dad keeps calling everyone, giving them contradictory instructions. No one seems to know what they're doing."

Eddie began walking, taking in the view. He was not going to get tangled up in this. "Tell Dad to back off. Stop bothering them, and let them do their job."

"Olga says they're in trouble."

Eddie sighed. "Mom, that's the nature of the restaurant business. It's always a bit chaotic. Give them a few days, they'll all settle down."

"A few days?" His mother sounded stressed, anxious. "We don't have a few days. Olga said if you're not here by the weekend, we won't have a business."

"Mom, I've told you, I'm not going to ride in like some knight on a white horse to save the business. That's not what it needs."

And not what I need either, thought Eddie, though he didn't say it.

His mother's voice went quiet. Eddie could barely hear her. "I'm scared, Eddie. If someone doesn't do something soon, everything your father has worked for these past 30 years is going to be gone. And Lord knows what that would do to him. It's his life."

Eddie slid his phone back into his pocket and gazed at the water, dark and deep, waves rolling relentlessly toward the shore. He knew what he had to do. It was the thing he feared most, the thing he had been running from all his life, but now he had no choice. He could either ignore his mother's pleas and let the business falter, maybe even close down, or he could step in. Return home. Face his father. Face his demons. He had made a career out of taking over businesses and reviving them, and he was good at it, but this would be the ultimate test. As a businessman he would never take over a business like this. But as a son, despite his protests, he felt duty-bound to do so. Saving his father's business would be the most daunting challenge he had ever faced, both as a businessman and as a son.

"

*The journey of
a thousand miles begins
with one step.*

LAO TZU

"

CHAPTER 2

All Is Not What It Seems

"Sir? Excuse me, Sir? Are you willing to assist in the event of an emergency?"

Another day, another flight. Eddie Jr. glanced up at the stewardess. "Sure, why not?"

Ironic, really. That was precisely why he was sitting there to begin with. His career had consisted of jumping into one crisis situation after another, like a firefighter running past evacuees and into the smoke and flames. This, however, was going to be unlike any inferno he had ever experienced before.

Sunday morning, and he was on his way to Toronto to help save another business. But this time it wasn't just any business – it was the family business.

It was no surprise that he was in Save mode. As the eldest of four siblings, he fit the stereotype perfectly, feeling responsible for anything and everything. He had been told his dark hair and sharply defined facial features gave him a serious and distinguished look, but going back to the restaurant made him feel like he was eight years old all over again. Growing up, he had watched the business have a grinding impact on his parents, which is why he didn't get to see much of them. Deep down, he couldn't help but feel as if they had picked the business over him. Regularly being the last one to get picked up at day-care late into the night would take a toll on any kid. In one of many frustrated, emotionally-fueled moments as a teenager, he made a vow to himself: *I will be different when I grow up. I'll never get into the restaurant business. I will stay as far away from this as possible.*

The pervasiveness of the family enterprise was never-ending. Every night at the dinner table, Junior would listen as his parents spoke about that day's problems. Conflicts with employees, trusted staff stealing from them, hassles with the Union, not being able to find good people...and the list went on. Then there were late-night calls when something broke down or when someone didn't show up. Even family vacations were tainted with the background of workplace anxiety and stress. Eddie Jr. could clearly recall the childhood anguish of having a picture-perfect vacation at Disneyland torn apart at a moment's notice with news of something gone wrong at the restaurant.

Although he was just a kid, Eddie knew there had to be another way. Another way to work, another way to run a business, another way to live. Meanwhile, he watched as his parents weathered the constant barrage of ups and downs as they strove to build a comfortable life for their family. Eddie often thought that his father seemed superhuman as he tackled all these issues, day-in and day-out, but since Edward Sr.'s recent accident, the old man's humanness and fragility had quickly revealed themselves like long-term wounds suddenly laid bare.

If Olga, the General Manager, were to be believed, since his dad's accident the restaurant had been plummeting like a jet plane in free fall. Sales were down, one of the restaurant's key managers had quit and a customer complaint had prompted an investigation from the health and safety board. The business was on thin ice. Any more bad moves and the entire business could be shut down.

It's absurd, Eddie Jr. thought. His parents had dedicated over 30 years of their lives to building a successful company, and just a few weeks of being away threatened to bring it all crumbling down. It was no wonder his dad had always worked as much as he had. The way he ran it, the place couldn't survive without him.

Toronto's Pearson Airport was loud and chaotic with people. As Eddie Jr. rolled his carry-on through the busy airport, he wondered if he had packed enough. How long was he going to be there? What was waiting for him at the restaurant? He stepped out of the terminal into the crisp Canadian spring morning, hopped into a cab and began to prepare his mind for the restaurant. His eyes were unfocused, his mind miles away as the highway carried him past industrial expanses and strip malls and into the city center, every mile bringing him closer to the inevitable chaos of his family restaurant.

When Eddie slipped into Michelle's, it was busy to the point of frenzy, with the rainy morning threatening to make it even busier. By the middle of the lunch rush, the classic French bistro setting with its white marble table-tops, matching tiled floors, and wrought iron chairs with padded white leather seats would be practically submerged beneath a sea of noisy humanity.

The waitress didn't know him, so Eddie was able to get a table in the corner, order a coffee and a sandwich and sit quietly to watch everything before anyone knew he was there. He needed a few minutes to catch his breath and adjust to the rhythm of the place before beginning work. So he kept his hat on, hiding behind a newspaper. If any of the staff recognized him the game would be up, and he would be dragged straight into the thick of battle.

The patrons came from all walks of life to chat over coffee, fresh salads and gourmet sandwiches. Today they formed a raucous horde. *Good for business, though not so good when the same people occupied tables for hours without spending any more money,* thought Olga as she stood watching.

Olga was stationed in her usual place, standing against the wall off to the side of the dining room, watching all the moving parts like a drill sergeant surveying her troops. With an eye to catch any misstep from the staff, she could zero in on inaccuracies in a flash and cut most problems off at the pass before they escalated into something more serious.

Olga had a small frame, but what she lacked in stature, she made up with seriousness. She didn't smile much and the staff never really knew what she was thinking or where they stood with her, which was exactly the way she wanted it. When she was around, staff members were a little more tense, a little more alert and extra careful not to make any mistakes. Nobody wanted to be on the receiving end of her wrath or criticism.

Olga looked down at her vibrating cell phone. When she saw the name on the display, she took a deep breath and closed her eyes for a moment before ducking into the back area of the restaurant. Nestling herself between two big refrigerators in the kitchen area, she swiped to answer.

The doctor's voice was quiet, even bland. *Is this expert trying to disassociate himself from me?* Olga wondered. *That's what they teach 'em – empathy without involvement.*

"Mrs. Ivanov, I have your test results and..."

His voice trailed off into the background as Olga flinched at the loud bang of a pot crashing to the floor. Yelling, as expected, soon followed. Olga peeked out from between the refrigerators at the kitchen where there was a bustle of noise, steam and fast moving bodies.

"You've got to learn, Julio, there's one way to do things around here and it's called *my* way! I know damn well what I'm doing for this joint." Darius, all six-foot-five of him, jabbed a finger toward Julio like a stage villain.

Darius towered over most people and had the solid, menacing stance of an ex-soldier. Though he was only in his late 20s, the wrinkles on his forehead and the crow's feet around his eyes suggested someone at least a decade older.

"You're not much of a leader if nobody follows you," Julio snapped back at him before whipping off his apron and throwing it at Darius' feet, his strong accent getting thicker and climbing in pitch as his anger mounted. Almost a full foot shorter than Darius, Julio was not the back-down type, nor was he the first co-worker Darius had chewed out.

Julio stormed right by Olga and out the back. The gunshot slam of the metal door echoed through the large kitchen.

Olga ducked back between the humming fridges, forcing herself to focus on the phone call.

"Mrs. Ivanov? Can you hear me?" said the doctor. "I must tell you, your blood pressure is alarmingly high."

No kidding, thought Olga. *You spend a few days here and see what it does to your blood pressure.*

"You are headed down a dangerous path, Mrs. Ivanov. You must do something about your stress."

Thanks for the expert advice, Doc, I'll add that to my to-do list. "Right. Uh-huh," muttered Olga. "I understand about the blood pressure." *Oh God, not Julio too,* she thought. *That's the third person to walk out this week.* More work for her, preparing another new job ad and repeating the entire long hiring process.

The revolving door again. Olga knew Darius was a difficult person to work with, but what could she do? It was hard enough to find busboys, that much harder to find someone to manage them.

From behind the kitchen prep table, the new Kitchen Manager, Tiffany Wilson, had seen the entire scene unfold in front of her. Given where she worked at the back of the restaurant, there was very little Tiffany did not see. It was her third month on the job and there had not been a dull moment since. In fact, she was thinking it was like one of those crazy culinary reality-TV shows with drama following drama day after day.

Tiffany's athletic build and quick reflexes gave away her past as a Varsity swim star, which had taught her a thing or two about maintaining her composure and working hard. She was hired by the owner, Edward Sr., a few months ago. When Tiffany started, Edward was omnipresent at the restaurant, but it had now been weeks since she'd seen him. Every day, she stood at her table and prepped food for that day. From leafy kale to meaty portobello and crunchy stalks of carrots, she methodically chopped away, watching and listening as team members gossiped, fought, and in some cases, stormed out in rage all around her. Amidst it all, Tiffany just kept her head down and tried in vain to block it all out.

The chaos made her think of a swarm of agitated bees buzzing around the nest when a threat appeared, and right now they were angrier than ever. She often felt her blood hammering inside her veins and wondered if it would lead to a heart attack. *I wonder how long I'm going to last*, she thought as her knife moved up and down, up and down.

*

Still fuming, Julio hurled himself into his car, slammed the door, cranked the motor and backed out fiercely in his battered red Honda Civic. He came around the corner so quickly that he nearly ran over John.

For a heavy-set guy, John was quick on his feet. His olive-complexioned face was contorted with shock as he jumped back with his hands in the air.

"Whoa – you tryin' to kill me or what?"

Julio slammed on the brakes, cursing under his breath.

John peered through the window and saw his nephew's beet red face. "Yikes. Who pissed in your cornflakes?"

Julio rolled down the window. "Sorry, Tio. Didn't mean to, you know…"

"I thought someone had taken a hit out on me," John said with a laugh. Then just as suddenly his expression changed. "Why're you leaving right now? It's the middle of your shift."

Julio turned off the engine. "Sorry, man – I did my best, but I'm done," growled Julio. "I can't work at a place where I'm disrespected. No way." He pounded his fist on the steering wheel, setting off the horn. "Not even for all the money in the world. I appreciate you helping me out with this gig, family and all, but nah, man, I can't do it no more."

John sighed. "Ah shoot, Julio, that's a real shame. You were good. Even Olga was pleased. What happened?" John leaned against the roof of the car and looked at his nephew. He was a hothead but a hard worker.

"That jerk, Darius, is what happened. Guy watches too much Gordon Ramsey," Julio said as he threw his head back against the headrest and let out a loud sigh.

"Ah, Darius again. Shoulda known. Anything I can do?"

Julio cut him off with a fierce shake of his head. "Yeah, right. How about getting him to treat people right. Think you can do that?" Julio shot back. His face was red with rage, the blood rushing through his veins.

"I'm a baker, not a magician," said John. He could see Julio's mind was made up. "I hate to see you leave, man," he sighed. "You've been good for the place. Maybe even good for me, but I get it. If it were me, I wouldn't be able to report to him either. I don't blame you - I'm just sorry." He paused and smiled. "See you and the family for dinner on Sunday night, right? Arroz con pollo?"

"Oh...yeah. Si, of course.." Julio's breathing was slower, and he wasn't twitching as much. He tilted his head and looked up at John. "You okay, man? You look like crap."

"Ha. Tell me what you really think. Yeah, I'm fine. Top notch."

"Spent the night on the couch again, huh?"

John nodded. "Yeah. It's all good, though – has me at striking distance to the kitchen." John gave a forced smile and a thumbs up.

"Sure, Unky. Whatever you say." Julio puffed up his cheeks and gripped the steering wheel tight. "I'm outta here," he told his uncle. "Time to go look for a new job. See you Sunday... And hey, all the best at home."

John stood and watched as Julio's car drove off, the faded red paint glinting in the sun, exhaust puffing and spluttering.

"Another one bites the dust," he muttered, shaking his head and exhaling. He twisted his back, setting off a chorus of cracks, and rubbed the back of his neck. *Time to get busy. From one battleground to another,* he thought.

*

Eddie looked around the meeting room. This was where the rubber meets the road, where his well-honed leadership skills would meet the reality of the restaurant. Would his techniques and ideas work here, as they had in every other environment where he had applied them? Or would his father's place prove to be resistant to good practice?

How many meetings had this simple room held? wondered Eddie as he pulled over a scruffy chair, the blue fabric torn and stained, and sat himself down. The microwave was pushing a decade at least, and the photos on the wall had been there since Eddie was a kid. There was a long table with eight mismatched chairs. Seeing it all brought back memories of sitting in on his father's meetings, barely eye-level to the table. His body tensed up as he remembered the intensity of those meetings, the shouting, the arguments, while he sat quietly trying to do his homework.

Now here he was back at the same table again, still feeling like a kid but looking like a grown man. Eddie watched silently as the management team drifted in one by one. The first to walk in was Olga, of course. Ever punctual, efficiency personified. *Here comes the backbone of the operation*, he thought. He'd seen that efficiency in her since he was a kid hanging around his dad's restaurant and had always been slightly in awe of it.

John was hot on her heels. He was also one of the originals. As Head Baker, he had the temperament of an artist with a passion for his dough. You could tell by how he handled it, moulded it, caressed it, that he took great pride in and cared deeply about his work. People swore his love-filled dough-handling – the joy, the energy – was a large part of what made the restaurant's baked goods so delicious. His department was an environment with plenty of heat. The bakers were a team of six men confined to a tiny workspace who began work around four every morning. Hot temperaments and shifts that started before dawn made for a crusty group who did not take kindly to criticism.

"Wow, little Eddie Junior- you have grown!" John said and laughed as he shook Eddie's hand.

"It's been a while, hasn't it?" replied Eddie. "It's great to come back and see old familiar faces and a few new ones. Welcome," Eddie said looking over at Tiffany and Darius with a smile. "Okay. Good people. I know since my father has been away there's been a lot happening..."

"Hey, man, is he okay?" asked John. "I can't remember the last time he's been away for so long."

"As you know, he had an accident and – well, he's banged up pretty good..." Eddie looked down for a moment.

There was a murmur around the table.

"Well, you don't have to worry about a thing here. We've got everything covered," said Darius.

Eddie looked over at the big manager and nodded. "Thanks."

John cleared his throat, raised an eyebrow and made eye contact with Olga from across the table. Darius was quick to intercept the exchange. "Got something to say, John?" he said in a voice that was more like a snarl.

John met Darius's fierce gaze. "Well, I don't know if *we* have it all covered. With Julio gone, I have to give up another one of my bakers to fill in for your department. That's going to leave us even more shorthanded and push my guys into overtime. That will mean that *my* labor cost is all out of whack. Do you know what it takes to make some of this stuff?"

"It's not my fault," said Darius with a shrug. "Guy was lazy and wouldn't take direction."

John sat up, his face flushed. "That's what you said about the other three guys. How could they all be bad? I've known Julio my whole life and he's as hard-working and loyal as they come."

"Really? Too bad I didn't see it. He was a waste of my time." Darius made a brushing motion on his sleeve.

John half-rose, but before it could go further, Olga spoke up forcefully.

"I agree with John that everything is not under control. We have had another complaint. Someone found a piece of plastic in their bread and we have been notified that the health inspectors could show up at any time for a surprise visit. We are already on thin ice because of the last incident. One more strike and they could shut us down." Olga grimaced a little. One hand fluttered up to cover her chest, then she quickly dropped it.

John sat straight up and frowned. "Wait, what -- who complained? That's impossible. Why is this the first time that I'm hearing about this, Olga?" he slammed his hand on the table.

Eddie leaned forward. "OK, John, take it easy." He looked around the table to make sure that he had everyone's attention. "The only thing that matters now is that we get our act together and pass this inspection, agreed?" He could see the suspicion in their eyes, but one by one they all nodded. "Great. Next question - why are we losing so many people? What's our employee turnover rate?" Eddie asked Olga.

"We're hovering at about 90% percent for the year," Olga replied.

Eddie couldn't hide his shock. "Wow - 90% percent? Are you sure?"

Olga nodded.

"It seems to be about the same ever since I've been here," said John. "Isn't that about industry average?"

Eddie looked around the room. "Is industry average really what we are aspiring to? Really?"

Silence.

"OK. Do we know why we are losing so many people?"

Tiffany leaned forward in her seat, her voice small, her words tumbling out as though she was afraid that she would be shouted down if she didn't hurry up.

"I've always heard that people leave managers, not companies." The room went quiet, and she shrank back into her seat. "That's just what I've heard," she said apologetically, feeling Darius's eyes on her.

"We are here every day, man," said John. "We work our butts off."

"It's worked so far, Eddie..." Olga said with a careful tone.

Eddie took a deep breath, knowing he had to tread lightly.

"I know," he said. "And on behalf of my family, I am grateful to you all for it. But one thing I want you to keep in mind is how much of himself my father poured into this business all these years. He was always here. All day, all night. Even when he wasn't here, he was working. He has always had it in his blood - his father had a restaurant back home - he was raised in the business. His efforts were the equivalent of four managers. Believe me, I witnessed it growing up. But I don't know when he'll be back, if he comes back. With him out of the mix, there's a big gap that needs to be filled, and between us - the five of us in this room - we need to figure that out." He could see he had everyone's attention. "I know how hard this job is and how much you all do," he told them. "Believe me, I'm not suggesting that any of you work any harder."

"So what are you suggesting, Boss?" John asked.

"Look, I've just arrived and I'm getting caught up. So far, looking at the numbers, I see we are replacing most of our staff every year, have lost a key manager, our sales are down and we are getting serious complaints that threaten our future. Is that a fair picture?"

He was met by an ensemble of nods. "These are all symptoms of bigger issues," Eddie continued, "and we need to get to the root of them."

He could feel energy coursing through his veins. This was what he did, what he was good at. "How much time and resources go into finding new people?" he asked them. "It's a huge cost. From posting ads to screening the hundreds of resumes that pour in, all the management time spent interviewing, reference and background checks, all that training investment. Think about how many new hires we have to go through to find a good fit. How about all the mistakes new hires make before they really start getting into the flow of the job? As you know, one bad experience is all it takes to turn away a customer, and an angry customer typically tells an average of 12 people about their experience. Think about how that is affecting our sales. Think about the cost, not to mention the energy, that gets poured into all that."

"You've got that right," said Olga with a sigh. "The never-ending story."

"All in, the cost of turnover is about $3,000 per employee - and that's being conservative. We have what, about 80 employees working here? Multiply that cost by almost an entire workforce that turns over in a year and then calculate how many pastries we have to sell just to make up for that cost. In the companies I've run, my goal has been to give people a home," said Eddie, "to create a culture that makes people want to stay, work from their heart and take ownership of their jobs."

John frowned. "C'mon man – these people are different. They don't care. They are here to collect a paycheck. It's a punch-in, punch-out job. We don't pay people enough to care. With all due respect, I've been here for many years. I'm not sure you realize the realities of this business today and the type of people who work here. Times have changed. Loyalty is dead."

Darius nodded along with everything that John said. "My guys clean dishes, wipe tables and scrub toilets all day long. You want them to care about that?" he asked.

"I know what it's like to work with a tough work force," Eddie told them. "The last business I took over was a failing fiberglass manufacturing facility where over 60% of our staff were ex-convicts. Their working conditions were terrible, but even at that factory we gave them a reason to care about the work they did everyday. They were part of the successful turn-around of that business."

Eddie had their attention. Right now they were prepared to listen to him, but for how long?

"I know what you might be thinking: the owner's son comes back after years of being away and wants to tell us how to do our jobs. I am not here to tell you how to do your jobs," Eddie reassured them. "You guys already know how to do that

- and better than I ever could. However, I can help you with your leadership style and teach you how to create a workplace that inspires and energizes your people."

He leaned forward, enthusiasm oozing from every pore. "Besides, have you considered how important your roles are? For many people, this is their first job. What they learn from you - how you lead them - will affect their careers forever. Also, people's experience at work has a huge impact on their lives. The environment you create here everyday is felt all the way back to the dinner table when they go home at night. It even affects their children," Eddie paused and looked down. "Believe me, I know that better than anyone."

Leadership style? thought Olga. *What on Earth is this kid saying?* She had to bite her tongue to keep from bursting out. *Sure, Junior. This is what happens when you get an MBA and come back with a bunch of bright ideas on how to run the family business. I'm just going to play along,* she told herself. *Give him a couple of weeks, he'll get bored or frustrated when he realizes how tough this really is. Two, three weeks tops.*

Olga forced a smile to her face. "Sure, Eddie," she said. "Let's give it a shot. Where do we start?"

"We start with this team. Let's all meet back here tomorrow morning before we open, say seven?" Eddie stood and gave his jacket cuffs a quick yank, his eyes darting around the room. "Everyone good with that?"

One by one they shrugged and nodded and drifted out of the room. As they headed out, Eddie could hear mutters and murmurs.

Once everyone left, Eddie sat down and slumped at the table, looked around the room and sighed.

What am I doing here? he thought. *Here I am, back at the very place I swore I'd never return. Maybe Olga had a point - business as usual had worked all this time, so why change now? Why should I stick around and fight an uphill battle that nobody even seems interested in? Why suffer through a thankless job to create an environment that nobody is asking for? How about when word got back to Dad about the meeting we just had? What would he have to say about what I'm telling his management team?*

That thought alone made Eddie shudder. He'd yet to see his father, had been putting it off, but sooner or later he had to go see his old man. What would he tell him?

66

*Enjoy the little things,
for one day you may
look back and realize they
were the big things.*

ROBERT BRAULT

99

CHAPTER 3

Gratitude Week

I t was a long first day at the restaurant. Eddie spent a lot of time simply being there and speaking with various staff members. There was so much he could learn from this casual chit-chat, or *MBWA* as they called it in business school: Management By Walking Around. That was a fancy buzzword for an otherwise simple thing - connecting to team members with sincere interest and curiosity.

Front-line staff are closest to customers and are filled with invaluable "data" from their interactions. While team members may not always realize this, asking the right questions will unlock a wealth of valuable insights they didn't know they had. Eddie Jr. had a head full of questions. How did people feel in their roles? What was working? What wasn't? There was so much to know, so much to learn, so little time. Eddie stayed at the restaurant late into the evening.

But that wasn't the only reason he was there late. Deep down, he was avoiding visiting his father. He loved his dad, and in so many ways they were quite similar - except how they thought about business. Once the conversation turned to work, that's when things quickly got tense. Eddie Jr. had experienced a lifetime of these arguments and really didn't want another. But as the last customers left, as the busboys locked the door and began stacking chairs onto tables, Eddie knew he couldn't delay much longer. It was time to go. With a growing sense of unease gnawing in the pit of his stomach, Eddie called an Uber. Watching anxiously as the little car with its icon approached, the minutes ticked down way too fast to his first meeting with his father...

It was dusk by the time he arrived in the old neighborhood. His Uber pulled into the small crescent road, veered around a group of kids playing road hockey and pulled into a driveway. The immaculately manicured front-lawn was lit up with garden lights, his mother's SUV parked in its space. Eddie sat for a moment lost in his thoughts and was brought back by the driver's eye-contact in the rear view mirror and his question, "This is it, right?"

"Yeah, thanks."

Eddie climbed out and breathed the fresh evening air, so welcome after a long day in the restaurant.

As he wheeled his carry-on up to the front door, it swung open to reveal his mother beaming at him as only a mother can.

Before he was even inside, she enveloped him in a big hug, the comforting smell of home cooking and rose water engulfing him, reminding him of his childhood.

As she pulled him inside, she unleashed a barrage of questions.

Have you lost weight?
Are you feeling ill?
Is everything OK back in Colorado?
Do you feel lonely there?
Maybe it's time you came home?

Eddie reassured her that he was doing just fine, that he'd been exercising more as of late, that he was happy. His mother gave him another scrutinizing look, clearly only semi-convinced, then led him into the living room where his father was laid out on the couch.

The family home was a clear reflection of his mother's personality. Cozy warm brown tones, soft leather couches and big fluffy blankets all combined to give the room more of a cottage feeling than that of a house in the city. The precise placement of every family picture, every plant, every decorative piece spoke of a level of organization that left nothing to chance.

Eddie looked at his father as he walked into the room. If you saw them side by side, their resemblance would be impossible to miss. Eddie gave his father a brief hug and felt the familiar bristly moustache against his cheek - a sudden and sharp reminder of the brusque greetings he'd experienced as a kid. That familiar, tickly feeling that he knew meant that his father loved him.

"So tell me everything," demanded his father. "How's my baby? Have they run it into the ground?"

Eddie sat down across from his father. "Before we get into that, how are you?"

His father was slumped on the couch, his leg in a cast from hip to toes. "It's nothing. A few more weeks I'll be up and running just like before."

"Dad, you're talking a broken femur here, that's not something you can just brush off -"

"Enough!" The old man cut him off. "You've spent all day at the restaurant. What's happening?" He pushed on without giving Eddie time to respond. "I heard they already got a complaint? Unbelievable. Can't leave them alone for a minute - someone's always got to be there or else everything goes to hell. Always looking for shortcuts. Always the easy way out. Do you know the hours I put into that place? Well, you'll keep them in line and show them how it's done, Son. I know you will."

Edward Sr. finally paused for a breath, allowing Eddie to reply. "I think they have a lot of potential, Dad. With some empowerment, some good coaching, I think they could really -"

"Empowerment?" His dad spat the word like an insult. "Don't waste your time, Son. I've known these people a long time. I love them like family, but there's only so much they can do. These are not the corporate-type people you're used to. They're like kids. You have to keep an eye on them, let them know who's boss, and everything will be fine."

Eddie bit his tongue. In his heart he couldn't disagree more, but now was not the time to have this argument. His father didn't seem to notice - just kept rolling on. "I think you can do great things here, Son - really move the business forward, help us with sales and marketing. Especially with all the experience you've had out there. It's good to have you back home."

Eddie felt his throat tighten. He didn't have the heart to tell his father that he wasn't there to stay. A family emergency - *a business in turmoil - a panicked mother* - that was why he was back. As soon as he could stabilize the place a little, he was out of there. Eddie wished he could connect more with his dad, but every time he tried, a wall went up. All he wanted to do was get out of there as quickly as possible.

"It's good to be back home, Dad," he lied. "I'm beat from a long day. I'd better head out and let you get some rest."

Eddie's father tried to get up from the couch to say good-bye to him, but Eddie could see that he struggled and his movements were slower. He didn't have the same gusto. Was it his injuries, or was his old man finally slowing down?

"Don't get up," said Eddie quickly, "I can see myself out."

His father sank back down onto the couch with a deep sigh.

"See you tomorrow, Son, and don't forget what I said. They're like children, stay on them."

As the Uber driver went through the neighborhood, Eddie felt a heaviness in his gut as he gazed out the window at the familiar streets where he had grown up. He replayed their conversation in his mind and thought about all the things he wanted to say to his father, all the things he felt he should have said. Yet he knew in his heart that if he had to do it all over again, he would say exactly the same things. If he was going to make the restaurant work, he was going to have to do it his way, and the last thing he intended to do was tell his father in advance. Better to apologize than ask permission, he figured, especially if you know for certain that permission would never be given...

*

At 6:58 the next morning, the team started filing into the break room. There was a quiet uneasiness as everyone took their seats, a few shuffles and whispers, but the team was clearly subdued, unsure what to expect.

Eddie sat at the head of the table on the battered blue chair that seemed to have become "his," a cup of coffee in front of him. He took a sip and looked around. *Here goes nothing,* he thought as he saw suspicious eyes looking back at him. *You've done this before, a hundred times,* he told himself. *You've got this.*

"How long is this gonna take?" demanded Darius before Eddie could even speak. "Cause we've all, y'know, got a lot of work to do."

Eddie took a moment to sip his coffee, gathering his thoughts.

"Good question, Darius. I know some of you came in earlier than your shift to join the meeting, so thank you for doing that. I also know that this may seem a little 'out there' for many of you. I'm grateful that you're willing to give it a shot."

"You didn't answer my question," muttered Darius.

Eddie ignored him for the moment. "My vision for this restaurant is to create a workplace we all love coming to every day. In the businesses that I've run, my objective has always been to create a working experience that leaves everyone feeling more energized *after their shift*, than when they first started that day." He made eye contact with Darius. "And all that takes is a few minutes each morning that will be repaid 10 times over as we start to understand how best to work together." Eddie looked around. Showtime.

"Have any of you ever been a part of a team that gave you a great feeling of connection?" he began.

After a moment with glances exchanged, John spoke up. "My high school soccer team in my Senior year kinda felt that way. We were really tight as a unit. We did everything together - on and off the field. We actually had the best record in the school's history."

Darius let out a deep breath into his mug that sloshed his coffee around. "That's what I miss most about the Army. The brotherhood. The connection and camaraderie with my fellow soldiers. We had a purpose. Can't say I always feel that here."

"Maybe if you –" John began.

Eddie quickly stopped him. "Thanks John. We'll have time for critical input later." He leaned forward. "I get it," he told them. "I've been there too, experienced that buzz, and that's what we're going to create here at the restaurant. First though, we need to start by creating that amongst us as a team. We do that by making time to meet here and have regular conversations together. This will be our Forum and there are a few simple rules I want you to observe."

He could see he had their attention. They may not be buying into it yet, but they were at least listening to him.

"First, we are going to establish what is called a vault of confidentiality. Everything we talk about is *Forum Confidential*. That means that nothing we share here can be repeated to anyone outside of this room. Nothing, never, nobody. Got it?"

"If we talk we die?" said John, cracking a smile.

"Exactly." Eddie continued. "We are also going to establish a culture of real-talk. That means we are going to say what's really going on for us and the business."

Olga scowled.

Tiffany squirmed in her seat.

These people are way outside their comfort zone, thought Eddie. *Good.*

"A tangible way of thinking about this is to think about sharing your top five and bottom five percent," he told them. "Meaning, we will share the parts of our experience that we are most proud of and excited about - the top five percent, and things that challenge us most...or the bottom five percent. The idea is that we want to talk about the parts of our experiences that are most impactful, whether it's the good, the bad or the ugly."

"Top five and bottom five with co-workers?" said Olga. "Seems a bit awkward, sharing like that..."

Eddie nodded. "Sure. But running a business is hard, and it's not always pretty. Kind of like a war. For us to have any hope of succeeding, we're going to have to do it as a team that's real with one another. We need to learn how to create an environment where we trust each other enough to speak up and say what's really going on, then learn to work with that. If not, then we'll never get to the root of the issues. This is a process, and we all have to commit for it to work. With every meeting, it will get a bit easier and it will come a little more naturally - assuming we all do our part to create a no-judgement zone here and always respect the confidentiality of what is said in this room."

"You've done this with other businesses?" Darius wondered aloud.

Eddie nodded. "And it works."

Darius wasn't letting it go. "What about a restaurant? Have you ever done it in a restaurant?"

"Not yet," said Eddie. "But all the same principles apply."

Darius settled back in his seat. "We'll see."

Eddie could feel Tiffany's eyes on him.

"Besides," he said, "on a personal level, have you noticed how much of our daily lives are spent staying on the *surface* of things?" Eddie smiled. "When people ask one another how they are doing, what is the typical response?"

"I'm good – I'm fine – doing great!" Tiffany said, in a mimicking tone. "But it's fake, isn't it? It doesn't really mean anything." She paused. "I guess I'm guilty of it too, but who really wants to hear your truths? Work problems, family hassles, personal stuff..."

"You're right, Tiffany. This has become the default way we interact with one another. We also don't want to dump the real story on anyone, do we? There's a time and a place to bring out the drama installments of real life. Well, together we are going to create a safe space where we can see what it's like to be just a little more real, a little more authentic."

Darius pushed his chair back from the table. "Whoa – what exactly are we going to be talking about? Besides, how do we know people are actually going to keep their big mouths shut?"

"Great question, Darius. I respect you for voicing your concerns – that's a good example of real talk. Look, truly, you don't know. That's why this is a process, a trust-building process. You will all have to earn each other's trust week after week. It's part of what we are learning: how to be discreet, how to protect confidentiality and how to withhold judgement. Will you commit to observing these rules?" Eddie looked around at them all. With a shrug here, a nail-rubbing gesture there, they all slowly nodded their heads.

"I will tell you this," Eddie went on. "Trust is delicate. What people share in our meetings must be dealt with very carefully. If someone does break this bond of trust and reveals information shared confidentially, that may be a breach you cannot recover from. I've seen it happen, so tread carefully."

All faces around the table looked serious.

"Okay – moving forward. At various moments, we will share our experiences, challenges and our successes with one another. You will be tempted to give ideas, recommendations or try to *fix* issues for one another. Don't – no matter how tempting. Your job is to offer an *experience share* – meaning, you can talk about how you can relate to someone's experience with your own. The only exception is if someone asks specifically for advice."

Eddie looked around the table at their blank faces and smiled again. "I'm going to ask you questions, and I want you to observe what comes up for you. Typically, my rule of thumb is that your first thought is your best thought. Your brain knows what it's doing when it rushes in like that and puts words in your mouth. So, when you feel moved to speak, share it with the group. Sometimes you may begin speaking at the same time and interrupt each other. That's okay. That's bound to happen at least a couple of times each meeting. The key is to share – courageously, openly and from your heart."

"Sounds fun," quipped John.

"I'm really looking forward to knowing more about each of you." Eddie looked at them, face after face. "I find the fastest way to get to know someone is to learn about what they value most. So, when you think about your lives, either at work, home or in-between, what are you most grateful for?"

The room was silent. Tiffany, who had developed a routine of writing in a gratitude journal every morning, knew exactly what that was for her: her family, of course. But as she opened her mouth to speak, she froze. *But what if that's too cheesy or not top five percent enough?*

The silence went on. Finally John spoke up. "For me, it's easy, man – I'm grateful for my family. I am so lucky to have an amazing wife and the greatest children in the world."

"Beautiful!" Eddie said. "What are you most grateful for when it comes to your family?"

John thought about it for a few moments. "Definitely their health. Growing up, my little brother had some serious health issues. God, it was terrible." His chin quivered a little in tandem with murmurs of sympathy. "It devastated my family, especially my parents. Long story, but never mind now. Thank God my own family is healthy. Having gone through that once, I feel like I've won the lottery with my family."

Tiffany's eyes were riveted on John. She quickly spoke up: "I have to second that – my family is everything to me."

"Tell us about them," Eddie said, leaning forward.

"Well, my husband and I met when we were 17," Tiffany started.

"How did you meet?"

Tiffany blushed. "We were actually paired together on a project in our chemistry class. Funny how fate works out, eh? My teacher practically decided my future for me."

"That's convenient! How did the project go?"

"Well, yeah, we definitely had chemistry!" Tiffany's cheeks were red by now. "We spent the entire time talking about everything but our assignment. We had so much in common, including not understanding much about the subject. So that project didn't work out so well. But the rest of it –" Tiffany's eyes were bright, her hands animated. "Well, neither of us will ever be scientists, put it that way."

There was silence and a few smiles.

Olga sat up straight in her chair, her shoulders pushed back. "For me, it's my grandparents."

"What about your grandparents are you grateful for?" Eddie asked.

"They raised me," Olga said. "I never knew my parents. They died in a car accident just weeks after I was born. So my grandparents *are* my parents. They're all I ever had."

After a moment John leaned forward and said sheepishly, "Jeez, Olga, hey, I'm sorry. I had no idea –"

"Of course you didn't. How could you? We've never spoken about it," Olga said.

"So what were your grandparents like?" asked John.

"Loving, caring...and also strict. They taught me discipline, responsibility and respect. Always kind, lots of hugs, but never letting me get away with anything." A big smile spread across her face, the kind of smile her colleagues had rarely seen.

Then the only person left to share was Darius.

"What does gratitude mean to you?" Eddie asked him.

Darius snorted, "I think it's all just a big waste of time, a way for lazy people to make themselves feel good, looking backward. It's the stuff you see on greeting cards. Y'know what I mean? Superficial."

Everyone stared.

"You've seen those cards?" John said and laughed.

Eddie narrowed his eyes. "Tell me more."

"Come on, man." Darius folded his arms across his chest and tilted his chair back. "Just sitting around talking about how great everything is, or the fact that there's other people in your life, doesn't give us much of a reason to get anything done, does it?"

"I hear that," Eddie said. "So tell me, what's important to you?"

"Work ethic," Darius said firmly. "Standards. Integrity."

There was a shuffle of feet, a barely-concealed titter from John.

Eddie smiled. "That's good. Different but good. We humans are complex beings. We all have beliefs, and no matter what others may think of us, we all have things that are important to us. So bearing that in mind..."

For the rest of their first meeting, they went around and shared, often haltingly, about the various elements of their lives they felt grateful for and what it meant to them. Whether with a hesitant smile or a frown, it was obvious this was not an easy process. There were muted exclamations, an occasional "Yeah," or "Good stuff," until finally Eddie heard what he'd hoped to hear: "Yeah...I can relate to that."

"Great - and it will only get better moving forward," he told them.

Looking round the table he could see that they were finally beginning to engage, joining in the conversation without always second-guessing themselves. He grinned. "Now for a little experiment. This week, as you go about your day, I want you to notice things you are grateful for. They could be big or small. They could be things you may not have noticed before. Your job is simply to notice them, then share them on the

Group Chat we are going to launch today. The bonus exercise is telling someone what you are grateful for about *them*."

"What if we can't find anything or anyone we are grateful for?" Darius asked.

"Honestly? That would be a first! If you just keep your eyes, ears and your mind open, you'll find something will pop-up and surprise you. Got it?"

Tiffany gave a big nod.

Daruis looked dubious.

Olga and John appeared non-committal.

"And then," Eddie continued, "Each time we meet, we'll take on a small activity or action that we will experiment with. It will rarely take more than 30 seconds to complete, so not having time will never be an issue. Your job, if we can call it that, is to do the experiment and then share what happened with the rest of the group. Have a great day everyone," Eddie concluded.

Darius noisily shoved his chair back from the table. "I'm grateful for this meeting finally being over," he said as he stood.

Tiffany shot him a glance then gave Eddie a quick smile as she scuttled out the door.

Once the room was empty, Olga approached Eddie.

"There are a few things we need to talk about," she told him.

Back into the trenches, thought Eddie as he refilled his coffee cup.

"Sure, shoot," he told her.

66

The word 'listen'
contains the same letters
as the word 'silent'.

ALFRED BRENDEL

99

CHAPTER 4

The Art of Listening

E ddie knew that his leadership style and what he was proposing was going to be a stretch for the team. For over 30 years, his father had run the business *his way*. His father was the Boss, the King, the one who was to be followed and obeyed. *Do as I say, not as I do.* There wasn't any room for brainstorming or collaborating. Debating ideas? HA. Now, what you really didn't want to do was question him - that would be a fatal mistake. It was his business and it was going to be run his way.

That said, Eddie had to give credit where it was due: his father was an excellent operator. He worked harder than anyone else, understood the business intuitively and was very good at what he did. He had built up a very successful restaurant starting with nothing. When there were issues or problems, everyone went straight to Edward Sr. and he'd solve them. It was no surprise then, that his father spent all his time at the restaurant fighting fires. He loved it. Loved the action - loved being the problem solver. It had become a part of his identity. On family trips, his customers would recognize him in airports overseas. He loved being the hero.

His father's approach was a far cry from what Eddie had in mind. He did not want to spend 70 hours a week at work. For him, there was more to life than working. Besides, what was he actually doing during those 70 hours at the restaurant anyway? Eddie believed in building a culture where people worked together and took ownership. He didn't care about being *the boss*. He wanted to build partnerships with his team. Getting everyone involved and to truly care meant the stress and the burden was spread across the organization versus shouldered by only one person. And Eddie truly believed that people did care. He believed people were wired to do their best; it was the role of a leader to create the conditions to help them get there.

But as Eddie was aware from bitter experience, it's one thing to establish this philosophy with a new group of people, as in a start-up, but a family business with a 30-year history of doing things a certain way is a different story altogether. Can a system that has been so deeply ingrained actually be changed?

Eddie pulled his phone from his pocket after he parked his car in the restaurant parking lot and scrolled through the Group Chat messages. He was pleasantly surprised by how quickly the team had taken to the Gratitude experiment.

Olga
I'm grateful for my friends and family 👵🧑

Darius
Pretty stoked our new puppy only pissed on the carpet once today 🐶...but the day's still short, so hopefully I didn't just jinx it.

Tiffany
Finally got to the pool for a workout ... first time in weeks!

Olga
Got lucky with the bus driver this morning. She waited a few extra moments to let me on when she saw me running!!

John
My Wife and everything she does for us.

Olga
So far - no surprise visit by the health inspector 🙏 🙏

Eddie was greeted by the smell of freshly baked bread wafting through the air as he stepped into the restaurant. It was already busy. The busboys set up the dining room chairs while the kitchen team prepped vegetables. Hot chicken noodle soup simmered on large stoves, the aromatic steam filling the kitchen as Eddie opened the door to the tiny meeting room.

Eddie watched as the team settled into their chairs, looking for any clues from their body language as to how they were feeling. Once everyone was settled, he pushed his coffee aside, held up his phone and smiled.

"Good morning everyone. Thanks for joining us today. You've done a great job sharing your gratitude experiment on the Group Chat. This morning, I want us to talk about what this experiment has been like for each of you. "John, why don't you kick us off. Tell us what it's been like talking about the things you're grateful for."

John fidgeted in his chair; he hesitated a few moments as he looked around. "OK, I'll go. Mine wasn't at work though. The evening after our meeting I was completely exhausted. I got home and just spread out on the couch, put my feet up and had a beer like I do every night. The house was completely quiet except for my wife working in the kitchen. Kids were asleep. I could smell stir-fry cooking, my favorite, and the sound of sizzling vegetables on the stove. As I sat there, I looked around and noticed the house was sparkling. I felt completely at peace and relaxed in my home. From where I sat on the couch, I could see my wife moving around the kitchen preparing dinner. I thought about how this was all possible because of her - because of all that she does everyday. You know, this is not the case for all families. Anyway, as I sat there, my phone buzzed. It was with a message Tiffany had posted about her workout or something, and it reminded me of our talk. That's when I sent my message to our Group Chat. I went for the double bonus points and I told my wife. I told her how much I appreciated everything she does for our family." John sat back, folding his arms across his chest. "So that's my story, anyhow."

"How did it go?" Eddie asked.

"Well, she looked at me funny at first," John admitted. "She asked me what was wrong and if anything had happened. Eventually she relaxed and man, I tell you, she has not been the same since," John added, shaking his head.

"It also doesn't seem like you've been the same," laughed Darius. "I've seen you yawning in the mornings, big man."

John waved Darius away. "I love my wife, and I am grateful for her - I always have been. But I realized it's been a while since I let her know. I figured it was obvious - that she knew."

"When was the last time you'd told her?" asked Eddie.

"I'm a bit embarrassed to say this, but I actually don't remember..."

Eddie looked at Olga. "How about you, Olga? What's been going on?" Eddie asked.

Olga sat up straight in her chair. "It's been good to think about the things I am grateful for. I realized that I forget a lot of the little things that are important. This morning, for example, while I was getting ready, it occurred to me that I was not in pain for the first time in a while - which is very nice for a change," Olga said, raising her hand towards her sternum and then dropping it.

"Why would you be in pain?" asked Tiffany with concern in her voice.

"I've been dealing with some health issues for some time now," Olga admitted.

"Wait, what?" John exclaimed. "What health issues? How come you didn't tell us?"

"It's not that big of a deal," said Olga quickly. "I don't like complaining. We've all got our own problems, right?"

Eddie glanced at the faces. They were all staring at Olga. He jumped in...

"It's amazing how little we may know about the people we spend so much time with day-in and day-out at work, isn't it? You raise a great point, Olga. Is there a difference between complaining and expressing how we feel - or otherwise put, being vulnerable?"

Darius shrugged. "Not for me. Whichever way you slice it, it's complaining."

Tiffany stared at Darius but said nothing.

"What do you think, Tiffany?" asked Eddie.

Tiffany looked over at him like a startled rabbit.

"Who me?" She took a deep breath. "Well, I guess, y'know, that there is a difference."

"Tell us more," said Eddie.

"Well, complaining feels more like negative energy, kinda like blaming someone or something, instead of just describing how you feel. My swim coach used to say that only victims complain - if that makes sense?"

"But what if what you're sharing is negative - it's something that's simply not good?" John asked.

Tiffany leaned in, her confidence growing. "Well, take what Olga just said. She wasn't complaining, wasn't expecting us to fix something for her, she was just letting us know. When you know what people are feeling, what's happening in their lives, good or bad, it helps to understand them better. Otherwise, how would you know?"

Eddie nodded. "That's well put, Tiffany. And Darius, I agree with you completely. Complaining is a waste of energy. Expressing the way you feel - without judgment however - will make it easier to let go of negative emotions instead of being stuck with them. It also means not having to go through something alone."

Eddie could see from their faces that they were thinking, processing. He pressed on. "Whether you acknowledge it or not, we can't help but experience our feelings. Grateful, anxious, excited, lonely. We experience these feelings, and only we know what's going on. Sharing feelings means letting others know what we are experiencing. We don't make it right or wrong and we don't necessarily need to explore or explain why we feel a certain way. How we are feeling *just is.*"

Darius just shook his head. "Is this the part of the meeting where we sing *Kumbaya?*"

He was met by blank stares.

"OK - so we've established that we all have feelings," he added. "That's terrific. But I was somehow under the impression we would be meeting to talk about increasing our sales and fixing our problems - like the upcoming inspection for example? You know, useful stuff."

"You don't think any of this is useful?" challenged Eddie.

"This feels more like a therapy session than a business meeting," Darius told him. "Where's this all going? We are here to work. Everyone knows their jobs and what we are here to accomplish. If everyone just did that, everything would be fine." Darius folded his arms across his chest and sat back in his chair.

Eddie looked around. The others were thinking, processing, but no one looked ready to jump in. Darius's outburst had drawn all the air from the room. Eddie leaned forward. "What you say would be true - if we were robots. What I'm hearing you ask is, 'Why spend the time to learn about each other when we are here to do a job?' Anyone else have any thoughts?"

John raised his hand.

"Go right ahead, John - no need to raise your hand," Eddie said with a smile.

"Right, of course...," John said with an embarrassed grin. He glanced at Darius. "Honestly, I've had the same thoughts as Darius, but I had an experience this last week that's got me thinking a bit. On Sunday, Olga was in an off-mood. She came into the bakery and was being very snappy," John said, avoiding eye-contact with Olga. "Anyway, this isn't the first time, and as everyone knows, I don't take shit from anyone. What we do here every day is very hard, and if someone gives me attitude, I'm sending it right back. Well, with it being Father's Day and all, and knowing what I learned about Olga's family history, I just decided to bite my tongue and let it go," John said, scratching the back of his neck.

"What happened when you two have butted heads in the past?" Eddie asked.

John gave a bitter laugh. "Oh man, it goes south real quick. We usually don't speak for the rest of the day - sometimes that can last for a few days. We even avoid each other. It's stressful. It makes everything harder and can lead to things falling through the cracks," John puffed out his cheeks at the bitter memories.

"When that's happening, what's going on in your mind?" Eddie asked.

John took a deep breath. "I hate it, to be honest. I have lots of negative thoughts in my head - why I'm right, why she's wrong, what I should have said, what I'm going to say next time, over and over again. Eventually everything settles down and we go back to normal. Until the next time. I bet if I had reacted on Sunday it would have happened all over again. It's actually pretty nice that we avoided that one," John said.

Olga looked up and chuckled softly. "Yeah, that's true."

"You helped avoid that one," Eddie pointed out. He turned to his left. "What comes up for you when you hear that, Tiffany?"

"I feel like John really heard Olga's story the other day and took it to heart. Since he knew more about her and what she could have been feeling on Father's Day, he could really empathize with her," Tiffany said.

"Right. Listening was critical there. Can any of you think of anyone else you know who is a good listener?"

"Yeah, for sure," said John. "Growing up, I had an uncle who was an incredible listener. When I spoke to him, it was like I was the only person that mattered in the world. He didn't even have to say it, but I could just tell he cared."

"How did that impact you, John?"

"I really trusted him. I mean, everyone did. He was by far the favorite uncle - the one everyone looked up to. He was the guy we went to when we had a problem."

"And did he help?" Eddie asked.

"I actually don't recall him doing anything in particular. He never said much, but he asked a lot of questions. Funny thing is, I always walked away knowing what I had to do. So, I guess it did help, somehow..."

"My grandmother was the same way," Olga said, her eyes widening with a warm smile that took over her entire face. "She didn't react or say much, but I knew I had her full attention. She hung off our every word. She knew exactly how we were feeling, too - even if we didn't say so."

Tiffany felt a tingle in her chest listening to Olga talk about her grandmother.

"Did she have psychic powers?" Darius sneered.

"Some people can seem like they do," Eddie said quickly. "What Olga is describing is called Zone 3 listening. It's when we listen to connect and are listening for what the person is expressing - what they are feeling. When we're in Zone 3 listening, we can actually feel what the speaker is feeling. And it doesn't necessarily take clairvoyant skills. Sometimes it's a matter of tuning in and connecting to what people *aren't* saying," Eddie explained.

"I've felt that before," Tiffany said quickly. "I feel it when my little girl comes home from school after a bad day. When I ask her what's wrong, she says '*nothing,*' but I can tell by the tone of her voice that there is more to the story."

"That would come in handy with my girlfriend," said Darius.

"So you might actually learn something useful here?" laughed John.

"How about this one," added Eddie. "Have you ever known someone to interrupt when you are telling a story even when - "

"Now that would be my brother," John exclaimed. "You can barely get two words in without him..." John trailed off, shaking his head and laughing at himself. "Must run in the family," he grinned.

"Perfect demonstration!" Eddie said with a wink.

"Yeah, just the way we planned it, right Boss?" John chuckled.

"So if that's Zone 3, what are Zones 1 and 2?" Tiffany asked.

"Great question. In Zone 1 listening, you are listening to reply. You are in your own head, putting all your attention to your thoughts instead of what's being said. When we are in Zone 1 we are listening to reply and are either preparing what we want to say next or just flat out interrupting without even being aware we are doing it," Eddie explained.

Tiffany went red. She felt like a spotlight was beaming down on her, as if Eddie was speaking directly to her, that he knew that she was endlessly mentally rehearsing what she was going to say and frequently lost track of what was being said to her.

"As you start practicing this, it's important that you aren't too hard on yourselves. We are going to practice neutral-awareness. You don't know what you don't know, and becoming aware is a big first step," Eddie said.

"And Zone 2?" asked Olga.

"Zone 2 is listening to understand. When we are in Zone 2 listening, we are hanging off every word the person is saying. It's as if we are in a tunnel with them - heck, you can miss a flight being in Zone 2 listening. Actually - I did once!" Eddie said, shaking his head at the memory.

"So here's what I want you to do," he continued. "Go about your day like normal, but when you are in a conversation with someone, try to notice what listening zone you are in. Are you in 1, 2, or 3? Your job is to spot it, and then report it on the Group Chat as soon as possible. Got it?"

One by one they nodded their agreement - all except Darius, who was staring at the torn safety notices that covered the notice board as though they were the most interesting thing he had ever seen. Eddie quickly made the decision not to challenge him. Not yet.

"Now - like I said, you are going to uncover some things about your listening skills that may be uncomfortable for you while doing this exercise. Go easy on yourselves."

"So how do you actually get into one listening zone or another?" John asked.

"Practicing neutral-awareness," Eddie responded.

"Why do you call it neutral-awareness?" Tiffany asked.

"I want you to be aware of yourself," explained Eddie, "but to stay neutral if you mess up and drift into Zone 1. We all have the tendency to scold ourselves when we mess up. But remember when your little girl was first learning to walk? Think about every time she stumbled and fell over, what did you do? Reprimand her?"

Tiffany shook her head. "Of course not."

"Right. I imagine you encouraged her and cheered even the tiniest little steps of progress. Well, I want you to take the same approach with yourself. If you're getting upset when you catch yourself not listening, or in Zone 1, don't sweat it. Let it go and try to do better next time," Eddie said.

There was a hard knock at the door, and one of the line-staff poked her head into the room.

"Mrs. Olga. Sorry to interrupt. There's a man here to see you. Said he's from the Health & Safety Board?"

The room went silent. Everyone watched quietly as Olga solemnly gathered her notebook and papers, stood up and made for the door. She nodded toward Eddie. "Are you ready?"

Eddie buttoned his blazer as he stood up and straightened his tie. "Wish us luck…" he said as they walked out.

"Luck for what?" Tiffany asked once the door was closed.

"Luck that we pass the inspection and they don't shut us down," John said resting his chin on his hands.

*

Eddie found the inspection was like a slow and protracted form of torture.

After a brief, courteous greeting with the inspector Mr. Abrahams, they began. Eddie watched closely as Abrahams toured the restaurant, peering into every corner, asking occasional questions of Olga and writing notes on his clipboard at regular intervals.

Abrahams wore a dark tweed jacket, thick, horn-rimmed glasses and a semi-permanent scowl. He moved at a measured pace, the rubber soles of his shoes squeaking softly on the tiled floor.

Eddie was usually quite good at reading body language, but neither Olga nor Abrahams were giving anything away. Both retained a stoic, passive expression throughout, and both were in defensive body postures - Olga had her arms crossed while Abrahams clutched his clipboard to his chest. Neither cracked even a hint of a smile when Eddie made a misguided attempt at humor.

The inspection lasted for about 45 minutes, but it felt like about four hours to Eddie. All he wanted to do was shout, "Are we finished? Did we pass?" but he bit his lip and followed along behind, feeling like a third wheel.

Finally, Abrahams made one final note and slowly turned to Olga. "Is there somewhere private we could talk?"

Olga led them into her office, a tiny space with a small desk piled with papers and just two chairs. Eddie stood while Olga and Abrahams squeezed themselves into the seats.

"So how did we do?" asked Eddie, sounding a lot more breezy than he felt.

Abrahams peered at his clipboard for several minutes before finally looking up. "Not good." He handed the clipboard to Olga, who devoured it with her eyes, flipping the pages fast to find the problem areas.

"Under normal circumstances, I would fail you," Abrahams said, directing his comments to Eddie, "but I've known your father for a long time, and I understand that these are not normal circumstances."

Olga had reached the end of the report. She looked up, the bags under her eyes dark and heavy under harsh fluorescent lights. "Thank you," she gasped.

Abrahams held out his pen. "Sign there."

Olga took the pen and signed the last page.

"As you can see, I've given you a provisional pass with an advisory note on several items. These all need to be remedied in order for me to give you final approval."

He took the proffered clipboard from Olga. "I'll be back in two weeks time. I expect to see a dramatic improvement."

"Yes, yes, of course," said Eddie, holding out his hand for a handshake.

Abrahams clutched his clipboard tight to his chest. "I'll see myself out."

As Abrahams shut the door, Eddie slumped into the empty seat. "Thank God that's over," he exclaimed. "At least we passed."

Olga bit her lip, scanning her copy of the report. "Passed? Is that what you think?" She held the report up. "Make no bones about it, we failed. It might not have looked like it, but he was being nice to us. If these issues aren't sorted - and fast - we're out of business."

66

It ain't what you don't know that gets you into trouble. It's what you know for sure that just ain't so.

MARK TWAIN

99

CHAPTER 5

Defining Leadership

Eddie
I'm just getting off a conference call with six other people this AM, and found myself in Zone 1 many times - some conversations are easier than others!!!

Tiffany
Last night during dinner time, we had a Family Forum meeting. We talked about the listening zones and the girls did great but leave it to my husband to establish a Zone 0 smh

John
I am right there with him @Tiffany!!

Darius
Suggested grabbing pizza and beer to my gf last night. She said "fine" but I knew what that really meant. Ended up being a pasta and wine night.

Eddie
@Darius - way to catch that Zone 3!!

Darius
Crisis averted.

John
@Darius 😂😂

Tiffany
Was in Zone 3 with my mom today. Best conversation we've had in a long time!!

John
Told my bro about the listening zones....now he only interrupts half the time. Progress!

Olga
I did my best to stay in Zone 2 & 3 today with the inspector, but there was definitely a lot of Zone 1 happening. Good news, they are not shutting us down...yet. We got a "conditional" approval. They've given us a report with what needs to be fixed.

Eddie
@Olga - we'll take a slow yes over a quick no any day. Thanks for the update and nicely done!! Let's all meet for our Forum meeting at 7am tomorrow to discuss.

Olga
OK confirmed

John

Tiffany
See you there!

Darius
Roger Wilco

When Darius walked into the break room on Friday morning, Olga was sitting at the table hunched over, studying a document. She didn't look up.

"How are we looking?" asked Darius.

Olga lifted her eyes, a tired expression on her face. "Alive to see another day."

Tiffany and John walked in chatting loudly, then quickly quieted down when they felt the mood of the room.

As everyone took their seats, Eddie wasted no time.

"Olga, let's start with you. Tell us everything."

Olga cleared her throat, giving Eddie a nervous glance. "The inspector was very strict. He followed every policy right down to the letter. We went from station to station in the restaurant. I was very nervous and kept thinking, *Oh my God, what if we fail.* When he asked me about our daily washroom cleaning log book, I didn't even hear him. Not a good time to be in Zone 1. At one point I told him I was very grateful that he was there to help us make our restaurant better."

"Nice touch," Darius said.

John's arms were crossed tightly across his chest as he leaned in. Tiffany chewed her nails.

Olga gave a brief glimpse of a smile. "Yeah - I think it surprised him so much that it actually helped. He seemed to relax - a little. He was going to dock us points for our bathroom cleaning logs but actually gave us a break on it. If he had, that could've been it for us.

"You came up big for us, Olga!" said John.

"Bottom line: we got a conditional pass. We have a few areas where we got docked points, including bathroom cleanliness, maintaining the cleaning logs, bakery area and temperature levels in the fridge. He'll be back in the coming weeks for another inspection. If we miss the mark on any of these areas again, no more warnings. They shut us down."

"Shut us down for how long?" Tiffany asked.

Olga sighed. "Who knows? We've never been shut down before. We got a conditional pass once a few years back, and I've never seen Edward so stressed. From what I understand, if we fail, they shut us down until we address the issues, and then they have to come back and approve it before we can open up again. Thing is, it sets off a risky chain of events. When they close a restaurant, they stick a big red sign on the side of the door. When the shopping mall gets wind of it, they may not renew the lease."

"So let me get this straight," John said. "They can come in at any time over the next few weeks, and if the place is not in good shape, they can shut us down? I can guarantee it will be clean when I'm on the job, but I'm not here 24/7. Then what?"

"That's why we need to get the rest of the staff on board - we can't do this on our own," Eddie said.

"We're depending on the staff for this? Wow - we're screwed," Darius said, throwing his hands in the air.

"If you don't trust your team to come through, they will feel it. Believing in people is like sunlight to a plant. It's vital for their growth," Eddie said.

Darius said nothing, but Eddie could see the doubt in his eyes.

"After our meeting, I want you to get your teams together and explain to them what's going on and what we need to do to pass," Eddie instructed. "Olga, I want you to take the report they gave you and do two audits a day on it."

Olga nodded. "That should keep us safe in the short-term."

"Looking forward," Eddie told them, "getting the rest of the staff behind us, getting them to really care about what's going on, is what's going to keep us on the right track." He looked around at their concerned faces. "Right now, in this room, we have all the leaders. I believe in each and every one of you - and know that you will come through, but I wonder, how do you each see your role as a leader?"

"To make sure everyone does their job," Darius answered quickly. "But I can only do that when I'm here."

Eddie thought for a moment.

"Early in my career, when I worked for Danone Yogurts in Paris, I had a boss named Thierry Bonetto. Working with him had a big impact on my career and development. Thierry would take time before and after work to coach me and give me honest feedback. I could tell he really cared about me and my growth, and that helped me be open to his critical feedback - most of the time. He showed a lot of faith in me - probably more than I had in myself at the time. When you think of a great leader, who you know personally, who comes to mind?"

John jumped straight in. "I had a boss once, Louis Frederico. Boy - I would follow that man anywhere."

"What made him so great?" Tiffany asked.

"You just knew he cared about you and he had your back - and it made me want to do the same for him. Not just me, everyone felt that way about him," John said.

"How could you be so sure?" Olga asked.

"With Louis, while he was my boss, he really cared about me as a person. He wanted to know about my family. And when I told him things, he remembered. He remembered everything," John said.

"I had a teacher like that in high school," Tiffany added. "I could tell that he truly cared about me as a person, not just a good grade. I never missed his class."

"I had a boss once that would really get into the trenches with us," Olga added. "He was always there side-by-side to support us. No job was too small for him to pitch in."

"How about you Darius?"

There was a long silence. Darius had a pensive look on his face. He finally shrugged.

Eddie pivoted the conversation. "What happens when we haven't had any good leaders to learn from?"

Olga was quick to respond: "We have nobody to model after."

"When it comes to a leader, I want to see someone who is going to walk the walk," said John.

"Someone who will support me and help me grow - someone who cares," Tiffany said.

"I want to know how I'm doing - no BS. Give it to me straight," Darius said.

"Any leaders you haven't liked working with?"

"At my previous job, we never knew what type of mood the boss was going to be in," recalled Tiffany. "One day he was happy and excited, the next day he could be down and miserable. However he was feeling that day would change the whole atmosphere of the place. What's worse was, we never really felt like we were one team. Even when things got really hectic and we could use some help, he wasn't the type to *get his hands dirty*. He'd often tell us to do one thing and then do something entirely different himself."

"Alright - so there's a bunch of different responses - what does that tell you?" Eddie asked.

"That we're all just making this up and don't know what we're talking about?" John said and laughed.

"I think leadership means different things for different people," Tiffany said, looking around for reassurance.

Eddie nodded. "Right. So bearing in mind that you are all leading teams, what do you think your people want in a leader? What do they want from you?" Eddie asked.

There was a long silence.

"So maybe the reason you don't know is because you have never asked?" said Eddie eventually. "But rather than guessing, I want you to go and find out. Ask your team members, what do they look for in a leader?"

Darius threw his hands in the air and let out a deep sigh of frustration. "Wait, wait - what happened to our issue at hand? What about the inspection and getting people to chip in and help keep the doors open? Shouldn't we get that sorted first and then do our little field study some other time?"

"That's exactly what we're going to do," replied Eddie quickly. "But we need the support of everyone, which means we need to know how they want to be supported."

Darius looked around at his colleagues hoping for some back-up. "Guys? Help me here. Am I wrong?"

"Why can't we do both at once?" asked Olga. "The more we get people on board, the more they'll be working with us to turn this thing around, right?"

John and Tiffany nodded. "Sure. Why not."

Eddie clapped his hands together. "Great. Let's do this!"

*

Eddie arrived at his parent's home early Tuesday morning. His mom's garden was in full bloom with lilacs, daffodils and tulips adorning big green hedges. Sprinklers left a haze of suspended mist in the air, catching rays of sunshine and creating a beautiful rainbow effect.

When Eddie walked in, his father was sitting at the dining table, looking sullen. Eddie's first thought was that he was having a particularly painful day with his injuries.

"Morning, Dad - how are you?"

"Fine - Eddie, just fine."

Years of experience fostered an instinct to know when his father was not in good spirits. Something was afoot and Eddie decided to cut to the chase. "Dad I have some bad news - I…"

"I already know Eddie - Olga told me." He looked up with a scowl. "How could you let this happen? A conditional pass? What will people think? Everything I've ever worked for will be ruined. What in the hell are you doing there anyway? What's the meaning of all these meetings you're having? You're taking the staff away from their work and it has now exposed us to a major catastrophe."

Eddie felt his heart sink and his mind raced. *I'm responsible? I just got here... I'm not even getting paid to do this.*

Senior wasn't done.

"Thirty years of running this business, this has never happened to me - and now." His father shook his head in solemn disapproval that pierced Eddie Jr. like a knife.

While Eddie knew this wasn't true, that this wasn't the first time the restaurant had gotten a conditional pass, there was no point in calling his father out - that would only make matters worse.

"I told you, Eddie. You need to be watching over them and making sure they're doing their jobs - not having these pointless philosophical conversations. Quit wasting everyone's time. For Pete's sake, these are restaurant workers - not Harvard grads, Son."

Eddie couldn't hold it in anymore. "And then what, Dad? I watch over their shoulder today, try to control their every move - and then what? What happens next week, or the week after? If the place can't run without you, you don't have a business, you have a high-paying job! How about a restaurant where people feel a pride of ownership for their work instead of you baby-sitting them?" He took a deep breath and kept rolling before his father could interrupt. "And by the way, these people do care, Dad. Have you noticed how eager and excited they were when you first hired them? People want to do well. We need to help them grow and be successful."

His father sneered. "So you want to spend my dime to build and train these people - for what? So they can leave and go work across the street for an extra $0.50 an hour? I've been down that road, Eddie. I've been doing this for 30 years - I wish you would recognize that and give me some credit. Son, in this business, if you want it done right, you do it yourself. This is not the time nor the place to train the future leaders of tomorrow."

"Then when is the time, Dad? You've become great at what you do because you've had the opportunity to try, fail and learn, over and over again. I'm not saying we should just let them do whatever they want. What I am saying is that everyone wants to be successful. We can help them learn to carry some of the stress of the business."

His father scowled. "Looks like I'll just have to get back in there and do it myself."

Eddie had heard enough. "No."

His father frowned at him. "What do you mean, no?"

"I mean no, you don't need to get back in there. You brought me in because the restaurant was floundering, and I'm fixing it - my way."

"With a bunch of meetings where people sit around talking about their feelings? It's a waste of time, and what's worse, it's taking them away from their work." He leaned forward, his face red, eyebrows knotted together in anger. It was an expression that Eddie had seen many times when he was growing up.

"I forbid you to hold these meetings. From now on, you stop all this new-fangled nonsense and do things the way I say. Do you understand me?"

It was too much. Eddie climbed to his feet, clenching and unclenching his fists. He just wanted to hit his father.

"No!" he said finally. "I don't understand, and I won't do it!"

He turned on his heel and headed toward the door. "As long as I'm in there, I'll do things my way, the way I think they should be done!"

He stormed out the door, his father's screams and curses following him all the way down the driveway to his car.

66

What is necessary to change a person is to change his awareness of himself.

ABRAHAM MASLOW

99

CHAPTER 6

How are you perceived?

T he following morning, Eddie still felt dejected from his conversation with his father.

"How's it going?" Olga asked as Eddie settled in his chair, a steaming mug of coffee in one hand, a phone and notepad in the other.

"To be honest, I'm feeling a bit frustrated by a conversation with my dad yesterday, and I didn't have the greatest night's sleep."

Olga fell silent, surprised by his forthright response.

Noticing her reaction, Eddie forced a smile. "Bottom five percent, right? But thanks for asking." He looked around the room. "How about you all? How did your conversations about leadership go?"

"My team members seemed taken aback and confused at first," said Tiffany. "But once we got into it, they had a lot to say."

John shrugged. "It was a bit all over the place. Everyone has different needs. But it's got me thinking about how to deal with people differently. Hadn't really thought about that before."

"So how do you think you are being perceived by your people?" asked Eddie.

"What do you mean by that? How we are being perceived?" wondered Olga.

"Have you ever had someone perceive you one way - but it was completely off-base?" Eddie asked.

"Yes - everyday - it's called resting bitch face," Tiffany said, igniting a burst of laughter from John and Darius. "Get it *all* the time."

Olga looked lost. "What does that even mean?"

"Well, apparently when I am thinking, my facial expression makes it seem like I'm angry or something. People always ask me why I'm so mad, even if I'm having a good day. It's a lot of fun," Tiffany said with a thumbs up and a big exaggerated smile.

"So you're not actually mad the whole time? Good to know," Darius chuckled.

"What does that tell you?" Eddie asked.

"I guess it means that what people see, they actually believe - they think it's real - even if it's not?" John offered.

"What's the risk with that?"

"We may be intending to convey one message but giving a completely different one?" suggested Tiffany.

"But you can't control what people think," Darius protested. "If we were going to do that, we would spend all day trying to take care of everyone's feelings."

"It's not about being controlling - it's about being aware of the impact we're having. What do you think the alternative is, Darius?" Eddie asked.

"Simple. People need to either grow some thicker skin or hit the exit ramp," Darius said.

"And how has that been working out so far?"

"Well - there's certainly been a lot of leaving," Olga said.

Eddie nodded. "Our employees are volunteers. They are here by their own will and can leave at any time, right?"

"The busboys have the toughest job here," Darius fumed. "We clean toilets, wash the floors and move big boxes all day. We aren't out there delivering food in our fancy outfits."

"The bakery is no party - let me assure you," John said defensively.

"And besides," Darius continued, "we're hiring from a pool of Millennials and Gen Zs - I mean what can be worse? Lazy, entitled, disconnected and always on their phones.'"

Eddie nodded. "I get it, being in a leadership role can be overwhelming - especially when having to deal with the emotions of others. I was blindsided with it once when I was running a manufacturing facility in South Carolina. Every morning, I walked the plant floor and said hello to everyone. One day, one of the guys came to see me in my office. He was visibly nervous and asked me what he had done wrong. I was so confused. I asked him what he was talking about. He said he wanted to know if he was going to lose his job. I could not get my head around it. What on Earth was he talking about? Eventually, I came to understand that in my morning rounds, I had not greeted him that day. And to make matters worse, I had a scowl on my face. I disclosed to him that my breakfast had not settled well with me that morning and it must have shown on my face, and I hadn't intended to ignore him. There were over 200 people working on the plant floor and our paths had simply not crossed that morning - nothing more.

But it taught me that as leaders we are always being watched, and all our actions are being interpreted, so how we present ourselves has a ripple effect, like it or not. The good news was that I had at least established enough trust for him to come to me that day so I could set the record straight - otherwise, who knows how long that would have gone on."

Olga nodded. "I can see how that could happen. There have been times your father has come in and I thought he was mad at me all day, only to realize later that I had imagined the whole thing. Throws off my whole day."

Eddie turned to the group. "How do you all think you are perceived by your people?"

Like the rookie who doesn't even know what she's doing, Tiffany thought.

John was the first to respond. "Somehow I think I know what our next exercise is going to be..."

"Wait - oh hell no! Don't tell me you want us to go and ask our subordinates what they think about us. I can think of many forms of physical torture that are way more appealing than that," Darius said, looking around the room for support.

"Close," Eddie told them. "But I don't want you to ask them what they think of you - I want you to ask them how you are perceived - there's a big difference."

"That makes me nervous, Eddie," Olga admitted.

"Sure. It would make anyone feel anxious. Who else feels that way?"

Everyone raised their hands.

Eddie raised both his hands. "I am right there with you. Here's what will help. Begin by telling them WHY you are asking them - create some context," he told them.

"For example, you can introduce the idea by saying: *I'm doing a leadership development training and part of this is based on finding out more about ourselves. So we are relying on a lot of honest feedback.*

If you feel uncomfortable, tell them! Let them in on how you are feeling. So maybe say: *I feel a bit awkward asking this, though I know this will really help me grow: How am I perceived? What changes can I make that would have the greatest impact on my success?*"

He looked around the room to gauge their reactions.

"I can do that," Olga said. "I am actually curious to hear what people have to say. You don't know what you don't know."

"That's true." Tiffany echoed. "What about asking people outside of work? Can we do that?"

"Who did you have in mind?" Eddie asked.

"My husband and kids. I'd like to know what they have to say," Tiffany said.

John felt a sinking feeling, but said nothing.

"That's a great idea, Tiffany," Eddie said. "You get bonus points for that."

"How about triple bonus points for asking the in-laws?!" Tiffany threw out.

The group roared. Tiffany blushed, looked down at the table and smiled.

Eddie waved his hand to get everyone's attention. "Before you go, I have a few tips to share." He glanced at his notepad and read aloud.

"In order to really make this work, begin by telling yourself:

1) 'I am going to accept anything the person says as their perception - not the truth, an attack or even necessarily a compliment. It's simply their perspective.'

2) 'I am going to express gratitude for their feedback.'

3) 'I will take notes, say thank you and let them know that I will process it for a week and then come back.'"

"I'm going to need a teleprompter to remember all that," Darius quipped.

Eddie slid a sheet of paper across the table to each of them. "Read this a couple of times. That should help, and it doesn't matter if you get the wording exactly right."

They all peered at the paper like high school students studying their latest assignment.

"Oh, and one last thing. As you think of people to interview for this experiment, someone may come to mind who you feel terrified to approach. You'll probably think: *No way am I going to ask that person.* Has anybody felt this yet?"

John and Darius raised their hands and nodded.

"They are probably the person you can learn the most from, so don't avoid them..."

As if I could avoid my wife, thought John, as he pushed his seat back and gathered his notes.

For the rest of his shift, John thought about the assignment. He spoke to a few of his guys and heard a mix of feedback - mostly what he was expecting and some that got him thinking.

While John was having conversations with his team, in the back of his mind he was nagged by a persistent thought: *What would my wife say? Why am I so afraid to ask her?"*

And then he felt a knot in his stomach as he realized he was lost in Zone 1.

*

Darius found Marco gathering supplies inside the big walk-in fridge.

"Marco, I need to speak with you."

Marco froze, like a kid caught with his hand in the cookie jar.

"Don't worry, you're not in trouble," said Darius. "I just need you to tell me how I am as a boss - how do you perceive me?"

Marco was holding a box of tomatoes. He put them down abruptly and frowned. "How do I perceive you?" Marco stammered. "Um - good - great - no problems. Why?"

"I'm in this training program, they are making us do this, and I'm just looking for some feedback. How you perceive me," Darius said again, feeling as uncomfortable as Marco.

"Everything is very good," Marco replied mechanically.

Darius persisted. "Look I know this is weird, it's weird for me too. But really, what am I like as a boss?"

"You're a good boss?" Marco responded, trying to get the right answer as he rubbed his arms to stay warm.

Darius took a deep breath, wondering what to say next.

Marco rubbed his hands vigorously. "I can't feel my fingers," he mumbled.

"Why didn't you say something?" They stepped outside and Darius tried again. "OK - what would make me a *better* boss?" Darius asked.

Marco's wheels were turning. "Well, you are the hardest worker I've ever known," he began. "It's just sometimes, well, some of the guys can be a bit nervous to approach you."

"Not easy to talk to?" Darius started. *It's not my fault you can't man up,* he thought to himself. His eyes narrowed, he opened his mouth to speak and then stopped and took a deep breath. The two men stood in a sullen strained silence.

"Ok - well, thanks for the feedback," Darius said finally.

Marco still stood frozen, eyes wide and mouth ajar. "That's it?"

"Yeah - that's it. Good talk," Darius replied, walking away.

Marco called out to him. "Hey, Darius. Can you do me next?"

"Do what?"

"What am I like to work with? What would make me better?" Marco asked.

*

Olga found Annie in the break-room on her phone. Annie was one of their best waitresses, in her mid-20s, with a thick auburn ponytail and a smile that could light up a room.

As Olga sat down, Annie glanced nervously at her.

"Annie - do you have a few minutes?" Olga asked.

Annie clicked her phone off and answered quickly. "Yeah, of course. Is something wrong?"

"Everything is fine - I was just hoping to get some feedback from you."

Annie said nothing, so Olga pushed on. "The management team and I are working on our leadership, and every week we meet for a Forum meeting and explore a different topic together. This week we are talking about how our team members perceive us. What impression we give - whether or not we intend it. I'm hoping you can help me with this?" Olga said.

"OK. But how?"

"Well, you and I have been working together for some time now. How do you perceive me? What impression do I give off?" Olga asked.

Annie looked down at the table, tugging nervously at her ponytail. "Well, I think you're a great boss, Mrs. Olga. I mean, I have no problems, everything is fine," she mumbled.

Olga opened her mouth to tell her not to mince words then stopped, realizing that she wasn't finished speaking.

"And you have taught us how to work hard and how to do our jobs well." Annie paused.

The silence seemed to go on forever - Annie fiddling with her hair, Olga wanting to step in and say something but forcing herself to hold off. Finally, Annie looked up from the table and made eye contact with Olga.

Olga smiled. "Thank you for saying that. What else did you want to say?"

Annie took a deep breath. "Well, we really respect you - it's just, well, some people are afraid to ask questions. They are afraid to disappoint you," Annie told her.

"Tell me more - this is helpful," Olga said.

"I just know some of the other girls, they can be a little intimidated," Annie bit her lower lip and looked around.

"What could I do differently that would have the greatest impact on my success?" Olga asked.

Annie looked genuinely surprised. "Oh wow. I really don't know..." Annie glanced up at the clock on the wall. "My break is almost over, I should be getting back out."

Olga sat back. "Of course. Thanks Annie, but just one last thing before you go. If you were my boss, what advice would you give me?" Olga asked.

Annie paced on the spot for a moment and then her face lit up. "More conversations like this. And we like when you smile, it makes everyone else happy too." She scurried out the door before Olga could ask her anything else.

Olga sat for a while trying to digest what she had just heard. When she had first started working at the restaurant, Edward Sr. had taken her under his wing. He was a successful businessman who had achieved so much and was loved by the customers. The staff did not dare disrespect him or talk back. She looked up to him. Through all the years working there, she had never questioned the way she worked and how they operated the restaurant. She had risen through the ranks, and now she had finally *arrived* and was running the place.

But these past weeks with Eddie, and now this exchange with Annie, had got her thinking. For the first time, she felt unsettled and unsure. Was it better to be feared by the staff or to be loved? Could you be loved and still be respected? What's to stop people from taking advantage of that? Where was the line? As the restaurant buzzed outside the cluttered break room, Olga sat alone, her head filled with questions that had no clear answers.

66

*You must begin to
think of yourself as
becoming the person
you want to be.*

DAVID VISCOTT

99

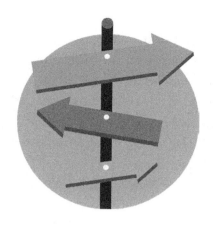

CHAPTER 7

Setting Intentions

The lunch rush was over. Eddie had spent the past hour standing quietly in the corner watching the staff going about their business. He was constantly impressed by how they worked seamlessly around each other, like a carefully choreographed dance performed at high speed with rarely a slip, trip or a stumble. Watching the staff, Eddie couldn't help but think about his conversations with his father. He was right, and his dad was wrong. The staff knew exactly how to do their jobs, they just needed to be trusted a little more, brought more into the running of the place so that they could learn to make their own decisions without always having to pass everything up the chain.

Eddie returned to the office and began reading through the Group Chat messages, his conversation with his father still running through his head:

He doesn't even trust me – no matter what I do.

He's so stuck in his ways.

Doesn't he realize there's a reason so many people keep quitting?

He doesn't even want to listen...

Eddie cleared his mind and tried to focus on what he was supposed to be doing. As he scrolled through the Group's messages, he read Darius's comments:

> **Darius**
> Spoke to Marco. Not gonna lie, it was weird at first but I think it went well overall. He hasn't quit yet, so that's good. Anyway, I need to work on being more approachable. Maybe I should bring my dog to work :-P

Eddie was impressed by Darius' willingness to step out of his comfort zone. It made him think of who he would solicit feedback from, and he was immediately gripped by a pang of anxiety. He knew exactly who he wouldn't want to ask how he was perceived, but once he thought of it, he couldn't unthink it. The mere thought of asking his father for feedback felt daunting, yet not doing it and being a hypocrite made his stomach churn.

He picked up his phone, opened his father's contact, then sat there and stared at it. *He was probably napping right now,* he told himself, so it wasn't a great time to call. He clicked off his phone and put it down.

What if it blew up in his face? Darius was right, physical torture *would* be preferable to going through with this. And yet... And yet...

He picked up his phone, clicked the number, and as it began to ring he prayed for voicemail.

On the third ring, his father answered.

"Dad - hi - how are you feeling?"

"I'm alright, Son - just lying down."

Eddie took a deep breath.

"Pops, I know our conversations haven't always been easy - well, far from it. But I'm committed to being a better leader and for us to work better together. I wanted to ask you a question. How do you perceive me as a leader? What change do you think would have the greatest impact on my success?"

There was a drawn out silence before his dad answered.

"You're always full of surprises, Eddie..." his father began. "I'm very proud of you, Son," he told him. "You have so often impressed me by what you've done. You have accomplished things I'd never be able to. But I wish you would be more open to my thoughts and opinions. When we talk, you get so worked up and don't listen to what I have to say. It seems like you don't care or respect anything I've done."

There was so much Eddie wanted to say in that moment. He bit his tongue to stop himself from jumping in. After a few deep breaths, he thanked his father and told him he was going to let what he said sink in and then circle back.

After they hung up, Eddie felt an array of feelings. From defensive to humbled, he did his best to just sit with it all. With his experience still fresh in his mind he opened the Group Chat.

> **Eddie**
> Just had my perception conversation. That was tough. Had to bite my tongue not to interrupt... so I was in Zone 2 - sort of. Anyway, gotta learn to be less reactive and more accepting of the feedback and experiences of others...especially when it's hard to swallow. #feelinghumbled

*

Another day, another meeting. As Eddie looked around the room he could see the beginnings of a different dynamic in the group. More trust, more willingness to listen, and an acceptance that the meetings were worthwhile - a part of their normal working schedule - not a waste of time or a distraction that was keeping them from more important things.

"To kick off this morning's Forum session, I'm going to ask John to read out our Forum protocols," Eddie announced. "Take it away, John."

"Ok Forum-mates here are the rules," began John.

▶ "Let's talk about our best and worst experiences - no middle of the road dilly-dallying.

▶ What's said here, stays here. So zip it.

▶ And finally - keep your advice to yourself."

Eddie smiled. "Thanks - John, I've never quite heard it done that way. I'm just going to add that advice is okay if someone specifically asks for it," Eddie added.

"Yeah - but people rarely do," John replied.

"Touché - ain't that the truth," Eddie said with a chuckle. "So, to get us going today, I want to hear what gets you energized at work" he began.

Tiffany was eager to start. "I like to peek out into the dinning room and see how people react to the food. It's a privilege to feed people - makes me feel like I have a purpose," Tiffany beamed.

Olga leaned forward. "I love seeing new people grow and develop from their first day on the job, whether they grow into bigger positions here or end up moving on to other companies. This is so often people's first job. I love being a part of that."

"I like when we're winning. When everything is running smoothly," Darius said.

"I've been enjoying connecting with my team more," John said.

As Eddie listened, he wished his father was a fly on the wall, hearing the passion and enthusiasm of this management team. These were the words of staff members who took genuine and personal pride in doing their jobs well.

"Terrific - how did the experiment go last week? I know this particular exercise is one of the toughest."

John nodded. "I'm glad you said that - I thought maybe I was the only one struggling with it. I noticed that people seemed to be caught off guard when I asked them. Nobody was expecting it."

"Yeah - Marco was straight-up trembling," Darius admitted, shaking his head.

"They seemed to want to only talk about the good stuff," said Olga. "I had to push a little to get the critical feedback. I learned a lot about what they weren't saying. Apparently, people are afraid to speak to me. Not sure how I feel about that," she admitted.

"They also said I was hard to speak to," agreed Daruis, "and that I'm always changing my mind."

"Who did you speak with this week, John?" Eddie asked.

"I spoke to my team-members mostly - and, I also spoke to my wife..." His voice trailed off.

Olga felt something in his voice and probed gently. "How'd that go?"

"Well, it was a tough pill to swallow. She said I wasn't very available to them. Even when I was home, I wasn't *really* there," John told them.

Listening to John made Eddie feel like he was reliving his childhood experience with his dad. "I know what you mean - I can relate in many ways," he admitted.

"What does that mean for you, John?" Tiffany asked.

"Well - I...." John started and quickly stopped, looking down.

The rest of the Forum members leaned forward. John was an exemplary manager. Always in a good mood. An employee of the month many times running, he was one of those people who could do no wrong. It was strange to hear him struggle.

John stared at his hands for a moment then looked up and met the friendly looks of his team mates. "In a way it didn't surprise me that much - but it was still hard to hear. I remember feeling the same way about my father - and swore it would never be me. And now look at me," John said.

"How do you want to be?" Eddie asked.

"I don't want to be an absentee husband, like my father," John said quickly.

"So how do you want to be?" Eddie said again.

"I want to be present and there for the people who mean everything to me," John said.

"Great - now repeat the statement starting with, I'm a leader who...." Eddie said, cueing it up for John.

John thought for a moment. "I am a leader who is present, supportive and attentive to those around him?" he suggested.

Eddie smiled. "Brilliant - now say it again, but as a statement you believe, not a question."

"But it's obviously not true," John objected.

"He's right," added Darius, holding his index finger in the air. "Heck, he even has a testimonial from his wife to prove it."

Eddie nodded. "I hear you. But let me ask you a question. When you are going on a trip, somewhere that may require a long drive, or a flight, maybe a connection, do you tell your friends you are *trying* to reach your destination?"

"No - I say where I'm going," John said hesitantly, trying to see where Eddie was going with this.

"Right - but what if the trip has an unexpected interruption? What if the car has a flat tire or a flight gets cancelled? Do you quit? Go home?"

"I guess any of those things can happen - but I'm still going to get there," John replied.

"Right - because you have decided where you are headed. Well - you've now determined where you are going as a person. You've decided who you want to be. Say it enough times, with conviction, and you'll get there," Eddie said. He could see Darius giving him a dubious look.

"Believe me, it works," Eddie assured them. "The brain can't tell the difference between the reality of who you are and self-talk about who you want to be, so either way it tries to act upon it. Bottom line, if we keep saying something positive as though it already exists, our brain tries to make it happen."

"And what if we constantly put ourselves down in our heads?" Tiffany wondered aloud.

"Same thing," agreed Eddie. "Ultimately, you'll become what you tell yourself you are."

"Then I'd better get this right," laughed John.

Eddie nodded. "It's important for all of us."

The group went back and forth for a while with Eddie helping to identify and clarify their statements. With Eddie's coaching and reframing they were gradually able to position their personal statement to reflect who and what they wanted to do or be.

Satisfied, Eddie settled back into his chair. "For the coming week, I want you to write this statement out on the group chat every morning," Eddie instructed.

"And then what do we do?" John asked.

"John, I think you *do* enough," laughed Eddie. "I now want you to focus on how you are *being*."

"How I am being," John repeated, nodding slowly. He paused and tilted his head. "I have no idea what you're talking about."

The laughter echoed around the table.

"I'm glad you're thinking that too," said Darius.

Eddie waited for the laughter to die down. "I want you to evaluate yourself by *how* you are being," he explained, "and not just on *what* you are doing. It's a tricky thing to explain with words because it's about the experience of being aware of yourself in the moment. When it comes to doing - you are all nailing it. All your hard work, the doing part of your job is what got you here. It's how you are showing up as a leader, how you are *being* that will get you to the next level. You come to work everyday, you work hard, you are getting it done. But *how are you being* when you're working hard? Are you inspiring and energizing people or causing people to become deflated and apathetic? Are you being alert or absent-minded? Supportive, grumpy or approachable? You could be doing all the right things and still the way you are being can have a negative influence on the environment - even if it's unintended. Leadership is about being aware of what kind of impact you are having on the people around you. Make sense?"

One by one they nodded.

"I want you to take the feedback you got and flip it around to define your leadership vision statement. John? Can you go first?"

One by one they repeated their leadership visions.

John: "I am a leader who is present."

Tiffany: "I am a leader who is confident."

Olga: "I am a leader who is approachable."

Darius: "I am a leader who explains things clearly and is aware of my impact on others."

Eddie smiled. "Great - now I want you to go back and share this with the people who gave you this feedback. Tell them who you are committed to *being*. This shows them that you have taken what they said to heart and are acting on it."

Darius looked around the room and grinned. "Well, crap, if we tell them that, then we actually have to do it!"

66

*Don't go on discussing
what a good person
should be. Just be one.*

MARCUS AURELIUS

99

CHAPTER 8

Being vs Doing

Text Message:

Olga
Eddie - can we talk?

Eddie
Sure - what's going on?

Olga
It's important. When can we meet?

Eddie
I'll come by the store in an hour.

Olga
OK

Can we talk? Those three words are enough to stir panic in anyone - doubly so when coming from the lynchpin of the operation. Eddie's mind swirled with what could be going on as he drove to the restaurant, wipers swishing back and forth across the windshield. The city was gridlocked as usual, buses and trucks and cars fighting for space - the usual traffic exacerbated by heavy rain.

Did we get another complaint? Eddie wondered. *Has Olga finally had enough and is planning on resigning?* Eddie shuddered at the thought. *What would he do if Olga left? Take over as GM? What would his father say? First the shop nearly gets shut down by a health & safety inspection and now his top general quits after 25 years on the job? So much for creating a cohesive workplace.*

When Eddie walked into the restaurant, it was buzzing with people and there were only a few tables available. Amidst all the chaos and change behind the scenes, business was booming. Eddie slid into a corner booth and took a few minutes to take everything in. He marveled at how Olga served customers, directed staff and all the while managed to keep cool.

The restaurant manager is truly like the conductor of a symphony, thought Eddie.

Olga spotted Eddie and hurried over to his table. Not one for small talk, she dove right in.

"Thanks for coming in, Eddie. I'm worried about Darius."

Eddie exhaled with relief - *Olga's not quitting!* - then tried to match her level of concern. "Tell me more," he said.

"He's acting out of character," she told him. "He has been abnormally quiet and has not been speaking or engaging with the rest of the management team very much. I have asked him how he's doing and he just answers with, *"All good."* This is typically what I see in people who are getting ready to quit. We don't have anyone remotely ready to replace him with."

Eddie thought for a moment. "Let's see if we can get a gauge for what's going on with him at our Forum meeting tomorrow," he suggested. "Whatever happens though, we have got to get a cross-training program set up to cover our bases. We always need to have someone in the wings for all positions."

Olga nodded. "Thanks." She stood, straightening her skirt. "Are you ready?"

Eddie checked his watch. Ten minutes to 12. Abrahams was due in at noon for their reinspection. "You tell me."

Olga looked around the restaurant. On the surface it certainly seemed to be running smoothly, but what about under the skin? What about all the little cracks and crevices that Abrahams would peer into, the hidden areas he would snoop around? "We've done all we can," she told him. "Let's just hope it's enough."

Eddie greeted Abrahams warmly and was met with the same blank reaction as before. Even with Olga's reassurance, Eddie couldn't help but be nervous as he trailed them around the restaurant, desperately trying to read Abrahams. Was he looking more relaxed than before? Was there the hint of a smile? Was the clipboard clutched a little less tightly?

If anything, this inspection seemed to last even longer than the first one, knowing that the entire future of the business was hanging on the line. But eventually it was over, and once more they wound up crammed together in Olga's tiny office.

Abrahams was in no hurry, taking several minutes to review all his notes before finally looking up.

Eddie found he was holding his breath waiting for the verdict.

"I have to say," began Abrahams, "that was much better."

Eddie gulped a deep lungful of air. They were still in business.

Abrahams leaned forward, handing his notes to Olga. "You've addressed all the remedial areas, and I noticed that almost everything seemed better than last time." He finally cracked a smile, an expression that seemed out of place on his usually stoic face. "In fact, I would go so far as to say that this is the best shape I've ever seen this place in." He signed his notes and handed Olga a copy of the report. "I don't know what you're doing here, but whatever it is, it's working."

*

When Eddie walked into the break room the following morning, Darius was already sitting at the table. Eddie did a double take. While Darius was never late to meetings, he'd never been the first one in either. The rest of the group filtered in behind Eddie. Tiffany began by reading out the Forum protocols.

"This is our Forum and our safe place," she told them. "Let's keep everything we talk about between us and challenge ourselves to talk about the good, the bad and the ugly.

Let's see if we can push past the top and bottom five percent and maybe even into the top and bottom four percent!"

Darius raised his hand halfway, then lowered it.

Eddie and Olga looked at each other for a moment and then at Darius.

He rubbed his face and looked up. "Of all the things we've done, this has been the most awkward yet," he admitted. "I just heard from people around me who say that I'm unapproachable and that I don't explain things well - and now I am telling myself the opposite? I dunno..."

John nodded. "I'm with you," he told Darius. "I felt the same way. My statement was: I am a leader who is attentive to the needs of those around me. Saying it, or writing it rather, felt like a sham. A few nights ago I was working in the garage when my wife came home. I noticed she wasn't in a great mood and when I asked her how she was doing, all she said was 'fine.' But I could feel something was up," John told them.

"Nice Zone 3 catch, John!" Tiffany exclaimed.

John flashed a quick smile. "Thanks - I've managed to screw it up so many times, it's nice to finally clue in for a change. Anyway, I knew persisting and trying to get her to talk wasn't going to help - been down that road too many times. So, I just kept my eye on her for the rest of the day. I would casually linger around, step in and help her with whatever she was doing and tell her how much I loved her. By the end of the night, she was in a completely different mood," John admitted. He sounded surprised by what he had said.

"So what do you take away from this, John?" Eddie asked.

John scratched his stubble. "Saying those few words in the morning kept me on track for the rest of the day. At first, I didn't know how I was going to actually do it - to be that kind of leader. But somehow, at the right time, I just knew what to do," John said.

"I second that," Olga said. "My statement was: I'm a leader who is approachable. I've noticed people have been coming up to me to ask questions or to tell me things more than before. It's not a huge change, but I've noticed the difference."

"Why is that important?" Darius wondered aloud.

Eddie looked around. "Anyone?"

"Well otherwise, they are too afraid to ask, so they end up doing the wrong things - or just don't know what to do and get stressed...which is often why people end up quitting," Olga said.

"Getting clear on how we wanted to be and show up has made a difference," John said firmly. "It's flat out working."

"It doesn't take a lot of effort to change the mood and environment of the restaurant - or I guess anywhere for that matter," added Olga. "Just feeling different makes everyone else act differently. Even just smiling more. I never realized how much my mood affected everyone else. It's kinda scary," Olga smiled briefly before reverting to her normal serious expression.

"What's the difference between what we *do* and how we *are*?" Tiffany asked.

Darius exhaled loudly. "That doesn't even sound like English - the difference between what we *do* and how we *are*, I mean," he reiterated.

"Doing is all the mechanical things we do on a daily basis," answered Olga. "We clean, we serve customers, we bake food. Being is *how* we do those things. We can clean attentively or clean mindlessly. We can serve customers pleasantly and make a connection or inattentively and see right past people. In both cases the customer gets served - but ultimately it's two very different experiences for everyone involved. Right?" she looked to Eddie for reassurance.

Eddie nodded. "Right. So think about your vision statements - how were you being, John?"

"I was *being* present and alert," answered John quickly.

"And what would be the opposite of that?"

"Distracted? Or pretty much the last 15 years of my life," John said with a nervous laugh.

Olga jumped in. "I was *being* open and accessible."

"Did being open and accessible require any physical effort?"

"No - not really. I didn't have to *do* anything - I guess I was just acting, well not acting, but I was being aware of it - and that made a difference," Olga replied.

"What does it take to be aware?" Eddie probed.

"Remembering?" offered Olga.

"I was *being* confident," Tiffany said jumping in. "I didn't even think I knew *how* to be confident - somehow though, this week, I just started feeling more confident." Now that she had started, her words came out in a torrent. "Honestly, I didn't even realize it until I said that just now. This past week I noticed there were times I was being timid and unsure in some situations. It got me thinking - *why am I being this way?* For a very long time - well, my whole life it seems, I've always felt like I didn't have much to offer and always needed to improve. Always felt like I have to work harder, learn more, do more, do better. By just choosing to be confident, I allowed myself to share what's really on my mind and show up differently." She sat back, a smile on her face. "I am enough. I have a lot to offer and what I have to say does matter."

Olga smiled and nodded in approval. "I've noticed it, too."

"Speaking of noticing," Eddie turned to Darius, "you were very consistent at typing your statement into the group chat every day. What did you notice when you did that?"

Darius stopped fiddling with his fingers, cleared his throat and sat up. "I'm not gonna lie, it was kind of weird to start. See, my statement was that I'm a leader that explains things clearly. So when I was training the new guy, Andrew, I thought about how I was giving him instructions. It made me think that so much of what I know is because of my time and experience here. But when it comes to training, I have been explaining things to people as if they had the same experience as me." Darius rubbed his chin and took a deep breath. "For a long time I've been looking for people who listened to instructions, who worked fast like me, who were disciplined. I've been complaining about everything and everybody. And I know why we have had such a high turnover among the busboys in my department. It's obvious now."

John's eyes were focused on Darius and where this was headed.

"I've been noticing how my guys have been responding to these little experiments we have been doing, and though I hate to admit it, how I am being is having an impact on others. They've been willing to do things more naturally - with less effort on my part. This is going to sound woo-woo or whatever, but it's almost like my team has been mirroring how I am feeling. It's a bit freaky though. I'm not good at maintaining it - I just keep going back to my old ways." Darius looked around as he finished. "At least, that's my experience."

"And what happens when you notice that? What's the voice in your head saying?" Eddie pressed.

"That I keep screwing up. It's freakin' *FRUSTRATING*," Darius said through clenched teeth. "I keep going back. One step forward, two steps back."

"What if every time you caught it, you addressed it with that neutral awareness we spoke about? What if I showed you a little trick that would help you with this? It may seem a bit weird, but it'll work."

Darius grinned. "I know you're going to show me whether I like it or not! Besides, everything we've done so far has been pretty strange - so why stop now?" Darius said, motioning Eddie to proceed.

"For the coming week, when you feel something come up, I want you to say hello to it.

For example, if you are feeling impatient, I want you to acknowledge it by saying, *hello impatience.*"

"You're right, that is really weird," Darius confirmed, shaking his head.

"You want us to say that...out loud?" John asked incredulously.

"Start with saying it in your head - or under your breath. For example, Tiffany, do your kids ever take their sweet time getting ready in the morning?" asked Eddie.

"More like when *don't* they," Tiffany said, shaking her head.

"How does that make you feel?"

"Frustrated, exasperated - homicidal.." offered Tiffany with a grin.

"In that situation, what would you say hello to?" Eddie asked.

"How about a psychiatrist," Darius mumbled under his breath looking down at the table.

"How about hello frustration and exasperation?" asked Tiffany.

"Right."

"Why are we saying hello?" challenged Darius.

"To remind ourselves that we aren't what we feel," explained Eddie. "When a strong emotion comes over you, by noticing it we see it for what it is - just a passing feeling. It's better for you to experience this for yourself without overthinking it too much. Like anything else, it may sound a bit strange at first, which is why I want you to try it this week and share what feelings you are saying hello to on the Group Chat."

Darius fidgeted in his seat. "Are we done? 'Cause I really gotta go say hello to number one!"

Group Chat from that evening:

John
Hello exhaustion - it's been a long day!

Olga
Hello Pain

Darius
Hello indigestion from too much nachos and cheese

Tiffany
Hello Child Services - please take my children away

Eddie
Hello excitement - I love hearing you guys apply this!!

66

*There are two things
people want more than
sex and money:
recognition and praise.*

MARY KAY ASH

99

CHAPTER 9

Praising Others & Ourselves

E ddie sat in his car, gazing at his parents' house. He hadn't been back long, but he already dreaded each visit with his father. At least he had the good news of the inspection to placate him with. He couldn't delay it any longer. Eddie pushed his car door open and marched up the path to the house.

"Your father's in there," his mother told him, gesturing to the study, "I'll bring you both a coffee."

Eddie found his father poring over the business section of the *New York Times*. "Stocks are falling," he grumbled as Eddie sat down next to him.

"Like you have any stocks," Eddie laughed.

"I have a few." He set the paper down. "So what's the latest disaster?"

Eddie reached in his briefcase, pulled out a copy of the inspection and handed it to his father. His father quickly ran his eyes across it and snorted. "That's a bit of luck."

"A bit of luck? Everyone worked their tails off to get this," Eddie said quickly.

His father looked unimpressed.

Eddie's mother appeared and set their coffees on the desk. "Are you boys playing nicely today?" she asked.

"Of course," Eddie told her.

"Always," added Edward Sr. He picked up his coffee, blowing on it to cool it down. "Tell me about our sales - how are we doing?"

"Our year-to-year comps are up," responded Eddie.

"And labor costs? I bet they've taken a hit with all your meetings and nonsense?"

Eddie met his fierce stare. "Down three and a half percent."

"So you are still having those meetings?"

"I told you I would."

"And I told you not to!" His father slammed his coffee down so hard he spilled it on the desk and across his hand. He sucked at his thumb while glaring at his son. "It's my business, and pretty soon I'll be back in there again. I don't want you changing everything and screwing it up before then!"

Eddie tried to bite his tongue but couldn't stop himself from rising to the bait. "Screwing it up? What part of sales up, labor costs down and the highest inspection score ever is screwing it up?"

"You know what I mean. Messing with people's heads with all that MBA stuff, all those touchy-feely meetings, people talking about their feelings instead of doing their damn jobs!"

Eddie stood up. "You know, Dad, I think you're jealous. Bottom line is, it's working, and you can't stand the thought that there might actually be a different, better way than what you've been doing." He stomped toward the door, then turned back. "I'm doing you a favor here. A little gratitude might be in order, don't you think?" Eddie stormed out, almost running into his mom in the hallway.

"What's wrong?"

"Ask him," mumbled Eddie as he pushed past her and out the door.

The sound of the door slamming was still ringing in Eddie's ears as he unlocked his car. He grabbed the handle, opened the door, then paused.

He'd made his point, sure. Shown his dad that he couldn't be pushed around. But what exactly had he achieved? How would it help in the long run, help in the ultimate goal of getting his dad back in the door with the restaurant running smoothly? It wouldn't.

"Dammit!" muttered Eddie as he stomped back up the path to the house.

If his mom was surprised to see him again so soon, she didn't show it. She just opened the door and watched him as he marched back to his dad's study.

"That's not what I wanted to say," said Eddie quickly, before his father had time to gather his thoughts. He took a deep breath. "I get it, Dad," he told him. "It's scary when someone else has different ideas, different ways of doing things - especially if they seem to be working. It makes you feel vulnerable, unwanted even." Eddie hurried on. "But if there's one thing I've learned working with so many different companies over the years, it's that the best bosses in the most successful companies don't do everything. They know when to sit back and watch and when to get involved and support. They let their employees get on and do the job and see their role as helping them to do their job, not doing everything themselves."

He finally ran out of steam and looked at his father. For the first time, he noticed how old his dad looked. Old and defeated.

Senior looked up at Eddie. "Thanks, Son," he said quietly.

*

Everyone sat around the table ready to dive in, like a group of hungry customers waiting for their meal.

Eddie asked Darius to say their Forum protocols.

Darius nodded. "Alright everyone, let's just keep it real. That means real good, or real bad, but either way we keep it in the vault. No snitching."

"That works," Eddie said, grinning. "Let's do a little update. What stood out from last week that you'd like to share?"

Tiffany barely let him finish before she jumped in, eager to share. "My in-laws were over on Sunday and they would

NOT stop making off-hand comments about how we were raising our kids. Not going to lie - I was borderline having a panic attack. Then I tried our little tool - I said, *Hello Anxiety* - and it helped. I mean, they were over *all day*, so I had to say it about 200 times!"

Eddie nodded. "Thanks for sharing, Tiffany. That's great that it helped. I recently had a situation that made me feel pretty anxious too," he admitted. "I said hello to feeling overlooked and taken for granted." Eddie looked around the room, swishing the coffee around in his cup. "Anyone else?"

"I know that feeling - especially when it comes from people who are close to us," Olga said.

John's face twisted with confusion. "Really Eddie? Guy like you and everything you've accomplished - I didn't think you needed it," John said.

"Well, you've done a decent job so far," Darius offered.

"Thanks...Darius," Eddie couldn't hide his surprise.

"It's true," continued Darius. "I mean, they haven't shut us down and nobody has left in weeks. Marco even said he liked closing with me the other day. He's a strange cat and all, but something must be working."

"That's great feedback. No matter who it comes from, being praised and acknowledged always feels good," Eddie told them.

"It's true," agreed Olga. "My grandmother told me that she was proud of me just before she passed. Nana said she was impressed by how I raised my daughters and how I worked through my divorce by staying positive and strong. I had never heard those words from her before about anyone."

"What would have happened if she didn't share that with you?" Eddie wondered.

"I would never have known," admitted Olga. "It was a very difficult time. I felt responsible and guilty about my failing marriage."

"Who would you want to express gratitude to - that you haven't?" Eddie asked.

"Definitely one of our lead waitresses, Annie," continued Olga. "She is so consistent, so dependable and it makes such a difference for me, personally. Whenever she's around, she helps change the atmosphere of the whole floor."

"Do you think she knows that?" wondered Eddie.

"I don't know - maybe?" Olga paused. "Probably not, actually. I feel bad saying this, but it's like I've just come to expect it. I guess I don't say anything because I don't want it to go to her head. Between us, if she left tomorrow, I'd be devastated."

"Same with my right hand man," said Darius. "The guy is so clutch."

Eddie looked around. "It's actually not that uncommon you know. Not to condone it, but let's get a show of hands of who else can think of someone in their lives who they truly value but haven't told them in a long time."

Everyone raised their hands, including Eddie. Eddie kept his hand up as everyone dropped theirs. "Just talking about this reminds me of where I'm coming up short here. I may be presenting this stuff to you, but I am no expert. It's a never-ending process. I don't say this to make you feel better, but to simply level with you."

"But doesn't this just come off as contrived and fake? Like we are checking the boxes by doing this exercise?" Olga asked.

"Not if it comes from your heart and is specific and concrete. Not just 'you're doing a good job,' but 'I'm impressed with how you are doing X, Y or Z'."

John almost raised his hand and then brought it down. "I don't know about you guys, but when people give me compliments, sometimes I kind of doubt what they are saying - like I don't fully believe them. Is that crazy or what?"

Tiffany's eyes got big. "Me too! I feel like people are just saying things to be nice or something. I don't really believe them." Her voice trailed off. "I thought that was just me."

John nodded in agreement. "I guess that's the good part about it being specific and concrete? That way you know that someone is not just trying to blow smoke up your wahoo."

"Nailed it!" Eddie jumped in. "That's what I want you all to focus on this week. Let's get out there and tell people what they're doing well. The formula for acknowledging people is simple: be specific, tell them how they are making an impact and start with the words *you are*."

"Praise everyone!" John exclaimed in a Gospel-singing tone.

"Eventually. But first, let's try it here together. I want you to acknowledge one specific thing about one another around this table."

"Oh boy..." Tiffany whispered under her breath.

"A volunteer!" Eddie exclaimed, pointing to Tiffany.

Tiffany went bright red. "I wasn't trying to go first," she said quickly, "but here it goes. Olga, you are a great trainer.

Those first few weeks you spent with me when I started made such a big difference. I was so stressed out, I probably would have quit if it weren't for you."

"Wow, it sure didn't seem like you were stressed," Olga told her. "You inspired me too. It's fun working with someone who is so eager to learn and do well."

"Great. Olga, you're up..." Eddie motioned to her.

She turned to face Darius, looking him square in the eyes. "Darius, you have been so engaging with your team members. We got a perfect score on the last health and safety inspection, and it's in large part because of your leadership."

Everyone nodded.

Darius furrowed his eyebrows. "Thanks, though I don't feel like I've made that much progress. I guess nobody has stormed out in the last few weeks - so that's good."

Darius turned to John. "Guess I'm up. John - you're alright, man. I know that even when I've been a real jerk in the past, you've always been pretty cool and chill. You've been a great mentor.

"Only in the past?" John said with a laugh. "Patience is a new virtue I am working on ....you've given me good practice," he said and winked. "I see a lot of myself in you - used to be just as much of a bone-head. You're doing just fine."

John turned around and faced Eddie and thought for a few moments before speaking. "I honestly thought all of this was a big crock of shit when you first arrived. Maybe I still do at times. But things are starting to feel different, especially at home. My wife and I haven't gotten along so well in - well, too long. I appreciate you, Eddie, for helping - with everything."

Eddie felt a chill of goosebumps on his back. He was here to help his family. He hadn't expected to have an impact on the families of others. Eddie was transported back to being a kid when his father came home tired, stressed and unapproachable. He wished someone had been able to work his dad through something like this. Eddie managed a half-smile, nodded and took a deep breath. "Thanks," was all he could say.

As the team walked out at the end of the meeting, Olga paused in the doorway. "There was one more thing I remembered about my grandma," she began.

Eddie put his notebook into his briefcase as he looked up at her.

"It was in her last moments when Grandmother told me how proud she was of me. For a long time, it had me thinking though, *How long had she felt that way? What if she hadn't said anything? How long would I have gone on seeking her approval?* I realized then that the greatest gift I could give myself was acknowledging myself - even if those who were nearest and dearest didn't - or for their own reasons, couldn't."

As Olga left the room, the tears that Eddie had been fighting back finally began to flow.

66

The greatest compliment that was ever paid me was when one asked me what I thought and attended to my answer.

HENRY DAVID THOREAU

99

CHAPTER 10

Leading with Questions

When Eddie arrived at the restaurant the following afternoon, he was surprised and dismayed to see his father sitting at a corner table sipping coffee, his eyes taking in everything.

Eddie hesitated a moment before walking over. "Hey, Pop. What's up?" he asked as he sat down beside him.

"Saw the doctor this morning," his father told him, "he said I'm ready to start getting out a bit. So here I am." He looked around. "Tell you the truth it feels kinda strange being here after so long."

Eddie said nothing and glanced around. After a couple of months, he was used to the rhythm of the restaurant and could tell at a glance when things were going well or when the wheels were about to fall off. Right now everything was running smoothly.

His father nodded. "It's looking good," he said finally.

Eddie nodded. "Yeah, it is."

Edward Sr. leaned forward, placing his hand on his son's arm. "I have to say, I was doubtful about all these meetings and stuff you were doing."

"I hadn't noticed."

"But seeing the place, talking to the staff..." He paused, struggling to express his feelings. "People are happy. Sales are good." He patted Eddie's arm. "You've done a good job, Son."

Eddie sat back, said nothing and allowed himself to bask in the glow for a moment. It had taken 37 years, but finally his father had recognized him, praised him. And boy did it feel good. "Thanks, Pops," he said finally.

Edward Sr. gave one more look around the restaurant, then slowly stood to his feet.

Eddie couldn't help but notice how stiffly he moved. "I think I'll head home now," said his father. "You seem to have everything under control."

Eddie replayed those words in his mind a few minutes later as he heard the raised voice of a customer from across the room. "I've been waiting 15 minutes for my grilled cheese sandwich and now that you've finally delivered it - you've given me the wrong sandwich," the man fumed.

Eddie was finishing his lunch near the front of the restaurant. He bit back the urge to intervene as he quietly observed the irate customer seething about the service.

The waitress scuttled off to get a Manager. Olga approached the man calmly and listened to him as he repeated his complaint, nodded as he spoke, apologized sincerely and told him that she would have been upset too if that had happened to her. The man calmed down, and Olga gave him a gift card and box of pastries as he left.

Eddie watched it all in silence, knowing he had his topic for tomorrow's meeting.

*

The next morning, Olga performed their opening rituals.

"What have you all been noticing?" Eddie asked as they settled in their seats, sipping their coffees.

"People like getting a pat on the back," John started. "Feels good to give it and people just seem more energetic and pumped up when they are recognized."

"I told Faye that she's really good at chopping the vegetables," added Tiffany. "Fast and accurate. I mean, you'd think that's a pretty simple, even dull acknowledgement, right? Well, she's been a vegetable chopping machine since. It's like the more you compliment something someone does, the more of that thing people will do."

"Exactly!" said John.

"I've even noticed it with my daughter," added Tiffany. "I told her that I was proud of how quickly she brushed her teeth and got ready for bed last week, and sure enough, the next few days, she did it even faster and was in bed *before* her bedtime.

I'm thinking of maybe keeping her after all," Tiffany said with a snicker.

Olga nodded. "I think talking about what is working tells people what's good and valued. It tells them what they should do more of. It seems obvious to us now, but people light up when they hear it."

"Guess we do seem to harp on the negative a lot. All the things we don't want," John began. He hesitated, then looked over at Eddie. "Eddie, I've noticed you are always asking us questions. Come to think of it, you never really tell us much."

"Yeah - what do you think about that?" Eddie asked.

Darius shook his head. "There ya go again! I saw that one coming though." He scratched his head through his short hair. "At first I found it pretty irritating. Like *doesn't this guy have any opinions or thoughts of his own?* But now I've come to see that it's better than being *told* all the time. I've actually been trying it with my guys."

Eddie was intrigued. "No kidding - how so?"

"Well, I always have to get on Mario's case about cleaning the dining room. It gets pretty annoying after the millionth time. So, I started asking him, 'How's the dining room?' First few times, I could tell I caught him off-guard. But now, he knows it's coming. So when I ask him, he's on top of it and proudly declares that it's tip-top. It allows him to have the win and I can give him props for it."

"I've noticed that our turnaround of the tables has been excellent," said Olga. "Was going to mention that actually. Nice job."

"So that's your secret, Eddie. Just ask a lot of questions and get others to do all the thinking. It's a lazy-style of leadership - I like it," John said with a smirk.

"You're on to me," Eddie said, holding his hands up. "I personally think it's more interesting to be part of the solution and share the victory. Feels better to help make the plays and get an assist than to always try to score the goals. What do you think, Tiffany?"

"When someone asks you a question, it forces you to think. I feel like I tune out when people talk at me. That's what I hated about school," Tiffany said, shaking her head at the memory.

"I've noticed that often when you've asked us questions, I've come up with answers I didn't even know I had floating up in there," John said, tapping his temple with his index finger.

Olga was conspicuously quiet and looked as though she was mulling something over in her head. "I see the point," she said finally, "and maybe that would work in an office setting. But when do we have time to do that here? This restaurant does over 15,000 transactions a week. I just don't have the time to sit there and ask questions. Doing something myself is usually quicker."

"That's what almost all business operators say, Olga, which is the reason why they never have time," Eddie began. "People who don't take time to coach and build up their people end up running around like chickens with their heads cut off trying to do everything themselves. They take on a small task here and a small task there because it seems 'quicker,' but it never ends.

And who is standing back and running the shop when they're so busy doing endless little tasks? So you're right, it does take an extra minute to pause and coach someone, but it quickly becomes second nature and pays you back a hundred times over."

Olga nodded thoughtfully as she listened to him.

"And speaking of this," added Eddie, "I overheard what happened yesterday with the gentleman with the grilled cheese who complained about his food taking too long. Do you mind if I use that as an example to illustrate a point?"

"Go ahead," Olga answered, though she looked less than delighted.

"Yesterday a customer complained about his food taking too long," explained Eddie to the group. "The waitress went and found Olga, who listened to the man, empathized with his frustration and took care of it. Handled it like a pro. So what's the issue?"

"I'm thinking that the next time that happens, the waitress is going to have to fetch Olga again?" Tiffany offered.

"And?" Eddie probed.

"Well, the waitresses aren't getting any better at it," offered John. "What if Olga's not there - or busy?"

"Yeah, but they probably can't take care of it the way Olga can," said Darius. "I think it sounds a bit crazy, feeding a rookie to an angry customer - just sounds like a bad idea."

Eddie nodded. "Maybe the first time. But there was an opportunity there for a training moment. Olga, how could you have coached her? What could you have asked her to help engage her in the process?"

"I could have asked her how she would deal with this? What would she do? But I wouldn't do it in front of the customer, right?"

"Right. But you could do it before and after speaking with the customer. It just takes a few extra moments to begin sharing your knowledge, to begin supporting her growth," Eddie said.

"So in the future, the waitress won't even need to get Olga involved, right?" said Tiffany. "She can handle it herself."

"Right. The greatest impact you can have is to develop others by sharing your experience and building them up," Eddie told them.

John nodded. "What I like about this," he said, "is that it makes us focus more on teaching than on always doing things ourselves. The more we build up everyone else, the more leaders we have and the easier all our jobs become."

"Yeah - but I'm not trying to be replaced," Darius said.

Eddie gave a soft laugh. "That's an age-old concern, Darius. Here's what I can tell you from the perspective of a CEO: if you can build up the people around you quickly, even to the point where they can replace you, do you think you'll be kicked out? There's no way. You're now a developer of people. The toughest part of business is having great talent and keeping it. Those who can build leaders from within are both rare and invaluable. And if the company isn't smart enough to give you greater responsibilities and rewards as a result, then believe me, someone smarter will - and they'll pay you handsomely for your ability to lead and coach."

There was silence for a moment as that sank in.

"So with everything we have been talking about, it seems the primary objective of our roles is to build up others, rather than the actual manual work we do?" Tiffany asked.

"That's what you have been doing with us all along, isn't it?" said Olga. "Training us to be leaders who can develop leaders?"

"That's it in a nutshell," agreed Eddie.

The silence this time was long and profound.

Eddie fought to keep the smile from his face. *They're finally getting it*, he told himself. *They don't know it yet, but pretty soon they won't need me anymore...*

As they filed out of the meeting room, Darius was surprised to see Julio waiting in the kitchen.

"Hey Julio, what's up?"

Julio glanced quickly toward John, who gave him a big thumbs up. "I was talking to my uncle, he said I should talk to you."

Darius towered over Julio. He took a deep breath. "Sure, what about?"

"John said things were kind of different around here than when, you know…"

A faint smiled crossed Darius's normally stern face. "Yeah, I guess they are." He gave a quick nod toward John and led Julio to the back of the kitchen. "You're looking for work, I take it?"

Julio nodded. "Yeah, if you're, you know…"

"We're always looking for good people," Darius told him, "and you're good - a hard worker. When can you start?"

John couldn't keep the smile from his face as he headed into the bakery.

66

Even though I had sold 70 million albums, there I was feeling like 'I'm no good at this.'

JENNIFER LOPEZ

99

CHAPTER 11

The Impostor Syndrome

E dward Sr. looked around the restaurant. It felt familiar, yet strange. His first full day back at work. Eddie had left the night before, and now it was up to him to take charge of the reins once more.

The staff began arriving, trooping past him, peeling off their jackets on the way in. Senior watched as they all headed toward the rear of the restaurant.

Olga stepped out of her office, her clipboard under her arm. "You coming?"

Senior scowled. "Coming? Where?"

Olga marched across the floor, her heels click-clacking. "To the morning meeting."

He snorted. "No." He paused. "Just be quick about it."

Olga said nothing, pushing through the door to the rear of the restaurant.

As the sound of her heels receded, the restaurant fell silent. Senior took a deep breath and looked around.

Unsure what to do, he wandered around, picking things up, putting them down, peering in corners and under tables.

Nothing.

Nothing was dirty.

Nothing was missing.

Nothing needed doing.

The sound of laughter drifted to him from the back. Senior frowned. More laughter. He started toward the back and hesitated. He started again, this time with more resolve.

"So what did your husband say?"

Tiffany laughed. "That's the funny thing. I had expected him to push back, but he just took it in stride and said -"

They all looked around as the door opened. Edward Sr. stood in the doorway looking like a little boy who'd lost his mother.

"Come in," said Olga quickly. "Darius, would you pull up a chair for Edward?"

"Yeah, course. There ya go, Boss." He slid a chair toward Senior.

He slowly lowered himself into the chair and looked around. "I thought I'd just come, you know, see what it's all about."

He was met with a room full of smiles.

"It's lovely to see you here," said Olga.

"We should maybe start by going over the rules one more time?" suggested Darius.

Olga smiled. "That's a great idea, Darius. Would you do the honors?"

After Darius had finished, Olga looked around. "I chatted with Eddie about what we were discussing the other day. He said it's called the Imposter Syndrome."

"That's a good name," said John. "I had it again the other day. I was working with one of the new bakers and instead of just telling him what to do, I tried to ask more questions. You know - get him thinking about how we do things. Well, we were going through how we mix the dough and would you believe it, he showed me something I hadn't thought of. I mean it wasn't ground breaking, but it does improve our process," John offered.

"What was surprising about it?" Olga asked.

"As the Head Baker, I've always felt like I needed to know everything and have all the answers. It didn't occur to me that solutions can come from other people - especially new people. If we're talking bottom five percent," John paused, "it made me nervous for my team to realize that I didn't always have all the answers. What gives me the right to be the boss?"

John stole a glance at Senior as he said this.

Tiffany let out a loud sigh that got everyone's attention. "That's basically the story of my life. Feel like I need to know everything and be prepared at all times. If I'm not and anyone finds out - I'll be revealed. I didn't think others felt that way too."

"Eddie said that most people do," Olga told them. "It's this deep fear that we are impostors in our role and that we'll be found out and revealed. Even Einstein had it *after* he won the Nobel Prize, apparently."

Darius nodded. "I hear you, Tiff. I feel that way too. I've always thought it's my job to know everything, manage everything, or else I don't deserve my role," Darius said.

Senior had been listening intently, saying nothing. He cleared his throat. "Can I say something?"

"Of course," Olga told him.

Edward Sr. fidgeted in his chair, leaned forward and stared at the table, avoiding eye contact. "I remember when I first bought the store, I didn't even know the difference between the salad dressings. I felt ashamed and, well, it made me work harder than anybody else." He looked up, and met their interested gazes. "If we're gonna be honest here, I have to say I'm feeling that way again right now. You've all been doing such a fantastic job without me, I'm wondering whether I should even be here right now..."

Olga smiled. "Thanks for sharing, Edward. It's kind of reassuring to know that we all feel the same, isn't it?"

Epilogue

Eddie sat in the lobby of Mike Campbell's office, still feeling slightly groggy from the red eye into San Francisco. He was in an ocean of potted plants and old magazine."

"Eddie? Good to see you."

Mike strode toward him, hand outstretched. "Good of you to come into town at such short notice. Your partner said you only got back this morning?" He led Eddie into his office. "Take a seat. I'll have Sandy bring you some coffee."

Once they were settled in, Mike looked expectantly at Eddie. Mike was in his early sixties, like Eddie's dad, and through several months of discussions and negotiations he had gone back and forth on whether or not he actually did want to sell his company. He straightened his tie as he sat down. He leaned forward. "I'm keen to know, what brought you here so quickly?"

Eddie sipped his coffee. "As you know, I've spent the past couple of months looking after my family's restaurant in Toronto."

"Yeah, I heard. Tough business."

"No kidding." He paused. "Thing is, it gave me some time to do some thinking, and I ended up thinking about you a lot."

Mike gave an uneasy laugh. "I'm not sure if I should be flattered or worried."

"You've gone back and forth on this deal a number of times," Eddie pointed out, "and I think I finally understand why."

"Enlighten me."

"This business is your baby. You've built it up from scratch. For the past 30 years it's been your life."

Mike gave a bitter laugh. "And the rest."

"How do you give that up? How do you give up your life?"

Mike sighed. "Damned if I know."

"And that's the point. It doesn't have to be that way. It shouldn't have to feel like you are giving it up. We're setting your business on a path for continued growth and evolution. Besides, a business shouldn't be your life. If it is, it's an obstruction, an impediment to the rest of your life. But giving it up makes you feel scared, vulnerable. And what will happen to your business after you sell it? What does the future of your company look like? What will happen to your employees? And how about your legacy? Will it continue to live on or be destroyed..."

Mike had been listening carefully. "You're not wrong," he admitted. "I've asked myself all those questions and more. And you're here to tell me that you're the man to replace me, right?" he snapped.

Eddie felt his hackles rise. This was just like talking to his dad. He bit his tongue, took a deep breath and carefully considered his words before speaking.

"I'm not here to replace you, Mike," Eddie said evenly. "I'm here to ensure that what you built, your company's legacy, continues to live on - just like I did for my family's business.

We're going to create an employee-ownership culture here where your employees will think, act and take responsibility like owners. We are going to create a stock ownership plan for your people which will allow them to participate in the ownership of the business. This is going to change their lives, Mike."

Mike raised an eyebrow. "You did that for your family's business? And your father just stood by and let you?"

"Well, the fact that he was laid up with a broken leg at home helped," Eddie said with a chuckle. "The business is doing better than ever and it doesn't require my father to be there around the clock anymore. Mike, this is an opportunity for a whole new beginning for your business, for the people who helped you build it. This is about passing the torch, about taking what you started and ensuring it endures the test of time. And besides, it's your opportunity to start the next phase of your life, to see what it feels like to not work 51 weeks per year. Not to get those 3 AM 'emergency' calls. Not to have that sinking feeling in the pit of your stomach when sales fall."

Mike looked at Eddie for a long time, then climbed to his feet and stared out the window. Silence filled the room. Finally Mike turned back around and held his hand out toward Eddie. "OK, Eddie," he said, a slight smile creasing his face, "let's take another look at this and see if we can make a deal."

Your Turn to Lead a Cultural Revolution

Thank you for reading Turnaround Artists. The purpose of this book is to inspire and empower you to lead positive change in your personal, professional and family life. Throughout this story, you have watched a team go through this process and successfully transform their business, and in some cases, their personal lives. Now it's your turn to lead a turnaround where you live and work.

To support you, we have developed an immersive online book club to help you bring this book to life and recreate the impact with your co-workers, families and friends.

www.turnaroundartists.thinkific.com

This course is perfect for:
- Company team members
- Developing remote-team culture
- Supporting post-merger/acquisition integration

How it works:

▶ Assemble 5-8 of your co-workers, peers or friends

▶ Together, you will read this book, one chapter a week, apply an action step from that week and then meet for a Forum meeting to discuss your experiences

▶ The program is 12-weeks long

▶ The process will cause you to build stronger bonds as you learn and grow together

When peers or co-workers go through the 12-week process together, this in turn launches their Forum group and is only the beginning of their journey together. These Forums always move on to new programs to explore together. Team members look forward to this special time where they can connect, learn and support one another.

Author's Final Conclusion

T hank you for taking time to read my book. Sharing my story has been challenging, passionate and fulfilling work, all at the same time. As you've most likely figured out, the story is about me and my family (my middle name is Eddie). When I pre-released this book, it stirred up a lot of conversations with others who had gone through similar experiences with their families. True to the theme of the book, it is a recurring reminder that our challenges in life are not exclusive to us and there is a feeling of great catharsis when we take the opportunity to connect on our shared experiences.

Everyone always asks, What happened to the restaurant? To your father? Is Olga okay??

The Forum has continued and is going strong.

The team from the story became so self-sufficient that my father stopped going in and eventually went on to start a new restaurant business. Interestingly, my mother - who always took more of a support role in the operations - became much more active, and thrived with the new philosophy and culture.

Month after month and year after year, the culture of the restaurant improved both in how it "felt" working there and also in sales and profitability.

In fact, the team got so engaged in the business that we went even deeper in the process. They were hungry to keep growing and to learn more. With my father gone, they took on more and more responsibility - like owners. I gave them a financial literacy course and talked about what it meant to think like an owner. How does the business make money? What really causes the business to grow? With these new Forum conversations, the team got to understand the impact of every action they took. They went on to create new Forums with the rest of the staff. Every day we posted the sales and costs results from the previous day. It became like a game to see how much better we could do together.

But given all the good things that came from this difficult experience, there are three things I am most proud of. First, our voluntary retention rate of 5.6% - this is the percentage of employees who willingly choose to leave their positions every year. When people leave, it's typically because they are moving away to another city or country. The number is so staggeringly low compared to the industry average (well over 100%) that nobody believes us. Secondly, the impact we have had on the personal and family lives of our team members. I've always said you can judge the culture of an organization by their winter holiday party. Ours gets a huge turnout, with family members and relatives alike joining with lots of laughing, drinking and dancing.

Finally, my relationship with my father. It has been far from easy, but I am proud of how far we have come and the relationship we have today.

Oh - and Olga is healthy and leading the business without disturbing her blood pressure.

Though I moved on to other businesses, we adapted our Forum process so that we could do it by video call. Word got out and we began launching Forums in the workplace for companies all over the world and launched the business Forums@Work (www.forumsatwork.com)

The mission of the organization is to make Forums available to the maximum number of people around the world.

There are three things I'd like you to take away from this book:

1) **To business owners and managers of people:** Practice these tools to the point where they become instinctual habits. You will discover an easier, more enjoyable and profitable way to lead your organization and teams. You can create a culture where your team members will inherently think and act like owners. This book is a step in that direction.

2) **To family business members:** Combining family and business is inherently an *extremely* difficult task that nobody can fully comprehend unless they experienced it first hand. You do not have to go at it alone. Join a Forum. Having the support of others who can relate will transform your life and will help others who are dealing with these same challenges.

3) **To the team members of companies who are unsatisfied with their work culture:** No matter what your position, you can make a meaningful impact. Applying the tools highlighted in this book will equip and empower you to make a difference. Over time you may opt to go work for a company whose culture resembles one we created in this book. Becoming a master of these skills will inevitably lead you to aligning with others who value it also.

Over the course of this book, we have learned:

1) How to establish and run a **Forum in the workplace**. A safe and confidential environment where people can share their experiences and relate to one another.

2) The power and practice of using **gratitude** to help us feel good.

3) **The art of listening** can be distinguished into three active listening zones.

4) The word **leadership** means different things to different people. The best way to know what people look for in a leader is to ask them. :)

5) Asking people **how we are perceived** and **what would have the greatest impact** on our success helps us understand how we are showing up and builds a new level of trust if we don't react negatively to what we hear.

6) Starting your day with an **intention** is a powerful way of leveraging our subconscious minds and our actions toward our goals.

7) Acknowledging how we feel by saying "**hello**" to our emotions is one of the fastest ways to shift how we feel in the moment.

8) **Praising** the positive actions of others will reinforce the desired behavior and encourage them to do it more. It also works when we praise ourselves!

9) **Leading by asking questions** empowers people to grow and become more self-sufficient by coming up with their own solutions.

10) No matter how much or what we have achieved, the **impostor syndrome** plagues us all. Relating with others by discussing our insecurities and challenges in a safe environment helps quell the inner critic.

About the Author

I was born in Tehran, and while I am a very proud Canadian, I embrace being a global citizen. I've lived in 10 countries and stopped counting those visited after numero 60 or so.

Today, I split my time between homes in Toronto, Denver, and Vail, Colorado.

I've never quite liked monikers or labels as I believe they are too reductionist, and I really don't like being put in a box. Turnaround Artist, however, I can live with.

A **Turnaround** for me represents a dramatic change in dire situations when there may have been little to no hope. It's fixing something others have given up on. It's inspiring new possibilities.

An **artist** uses creativity and resourcefulness to create something exceptional. In this case, to succeed where others have given up. While every situation is different, fundamentals are always the same. It always starts with leading, engaging, and inspiring people.

On a more personal front, I am a dedicated Vipassana meditator and have sat or served at least one 10-day silent meditation retreat every year for the last 10 years. I credit this experience for helping me cultivate patience, concentration and deep empathy. It is the best decision and single most impactful thing I do every year.

My interests and sense of curiosity have no bounds. I am a cinéphile, crazy about musical theater, will rarely turn down seeing live music, an avid skier and plan to always be learning a new language.

My Mission

My mission in life is to help create more employee-owned companies and employee-owners.

I believe the way to reduce the wealth inequality gap, empower people and to strengthen our society is to train team members to think and act like owners, create an environment where they can thrive and offer accessible opportunities for them to have a piece of the action.

The first step towards a company becoming employee-owned is creating workplace environments that are energizing because people can create and collaborate with one another harmoniously. I'm the Managing Director of a company called **Core Work Capital** that helps businesses become employee-owned.

Acknowledgements

The act of acknowledgement is so vital, it has its own Chapter in the book.

Firstly, I am grateful to my parents who have been a steady source of support, encouragement and love. The lessons, love and great memories far outweigh the bumps in the road.

Merci for everything.

I am grateful to all the people I have worked with in my career. From the mentors, the people I reported to and my direct reports. This book chronicles all that I have learned from our time together. Thank you for being part of my journey and thank you for your patience and understanding as I worked through my personal leadership development.

A big thank you to my editor Don Mcnab-Stark. While I feel lucky to have found you, I did have to interview over 50 people to track you down! You went above and beyond and were instrumental in making this book what it is today. Really enjoyed our collaboration - you are awesome!

A special thanks to the exceptionally talented Chiara Ghigliazza for the beautiful illustrations both on the cover and the icons for each chapter. A big thank you to Eled Cernik for your elegant design and layout work - really enjoyed working with you. Thank you to Adiat Junaid, Winnie Czulinski & Erin Zimmer for your coaching and support. It takes a village!

You have all helped me become a better version of myself.

Finally, a deep gratitude to my *writing spots* and the people who knowingly or unwittingly inspired me along the way. From my balcony in Toronto, to creekside in Vail, Colorado; walking by the duomo in Florence everyday on my way to the co-working space and the inviting inlets of Ischia, Italy. Odessa, Ukraine allowed me to get away from everyone and experience a brand new culture, the liveliness of Majorca and Barcelona, Spain helped keep the energy up and just about all the Soho Houses across London where the buffets fueled my rewrites. Finally, Paris, France where, with the help of a few strong ones, I finished the book by writing the book's first scene at Hemingway's Bar in the Ritz-Carlton Hotel.

The feeling and inspiration of all these people and places are contained within these pages.

Thank you!